2016

Preliminary Overview of the Economies
of Latin America and the Caribbean

UNITED NATIONS

ECLAC

Alicia Bárcena
Executive Secretary

Antonio Prado
Deputy Executive Secretary

Daniel Titelman
Chief, Economic Development Division

Ricardo Pérez
Chief, Publications and Web Services Division

The *Preliminary Overview of the Economies of Latin America and the Caribbean* is an annual publication prepared by the Economic Development Division of the Economic Commission for Latin America and the Caribbean (ECLAC). This 2016 edition was prepared under the supervision of Daniel Titelman, Chief of the Division, while Jürgen Weller, Senior Economic Affairs Officer, was responsible for its overall coordination.

In the preparation of this edition, the Economic Development Division was assisted by the Statistics Division, the ECLAC subregional headquarters in Mexico City and Port of Spain, and the Commission's country offices in Bogota, Brasilia, Buenos Aires, Montevideo and Washington, D.C.

The regional report was prepared by Daniel Titelman with inputs provided by the following exerts: Cecilia Vera, Claudia de Camino and José Antonio Sánchez (global economic trends and external sector), Claudio Aravena (economic activity), Ramón Pineda (prices), Jürgen Weller (employment and wages), Ricardo Martner, Michael Hanni and Ivonne González (fiscal policy), and Ramón Pineda, Rodrigo Cárcamo and Alejandra Acevedo (monetary and exchange-rate policies). Pablo Carvallo, Cecilia Vera, Alejandra Acevedo and Claudio Aravena were responsible for the economic projections, with input from the ECLAC subregional headquarters and national offices. Alejandra Acevedo, Alda Díaz, Fernando Villanueva and María José Zambrano were responsible for the processing and presentation of the statistical data and graphical presentations.

The country notes are based on studies conducted by the following experts: Anahí Amar and Daniel Vega (Argentina), Michael Hendrickson (Bahamas and Belize), Nyasha Skerrette (Barbados), Claudia de Camino (Plurinational State of Bolivia), Carlos Mussi (Brazil), Esteban Pérez (Chile), Olga Lucía Acosta, Yaddi Miranda, Juan Carlos Ramírez and Tomás Concha (Colombia), Ramón Padilla (Costa Rica), Indira Romero (Cuba), Cornelia Kaldewei (Ecuador), Stefanie Garry (El Salvador (with Jesús Santamaría) and Guatemala), Sheldon McLean (Eastern Caribbean Monetary Union and Guyana), Randolph Gilbert (Haiti), Cameron Daneshvar (Dominican Republic and Honduras), Dillon Alleyne (Jamaica), Juan Carlos Rivas (Mexico), Francisco Villarreal (Nicaragua), Rodolfo Minzer (Panama), Sonia Gontero (Paraguay), Rodrigo Cárcamo (Peru), Machel Pantin (Suriname and Trinidad and Tobago), and Álvaro Lalanne and Martín Brum (Uruguay). Michael Hanni and José Luis Germán reviewed the Caribbean country notes. Juan Pablo Jiménez collaborated in the review of the country notes for the Latin American countries.

United Nations publication

ISBN: 978-92-1-121938-8 (print)

ISBN: 978-92-1-058574-3 (pdf)

ISBN: 978-92-1-358050-9 (ePub)

Sales No.: E.17.II.G.2

LC/G.2698-P

Copyright © United Nations, 2016

All rights reserved

Printed at United Nations, Santiago

S.16-01332

Explanatory notes

- Three dots (…) indicate that data are missing, are not available or are not separately reported.
- A dash (-) indicates that the amount is nil or negligible.
- A full stop (.) is used to indicate decimals.
- The word "dollars" refers to United States dollars unless otherwise specified.
- A slash (/) between years (e.g., 2013/2014) indicates a 12-month period falling between the two years.
- Individual figures and percentages in tables may not always add up to the corresponding total due to rounding.

This publication should be cited as: Economic Commission for Latin America and the Caribbean (ECLAC), *Preliminary Overview of the Economies of Latin America and the Caribbean, 2016* (LC/G.2698-P), Santiago, 2016.

Figures

Box

Executive summary

A. Global economic trends

In 2016 the global economy maintained the slow growth trend seen over the past eight years, with a rate of 2.2%, the lowest since the international financial crisis of 2008-2009. As in previous years, growth was driven by the developing economies, which posted a rate of 3.6% as a group in 2016, while the developed economies expanded by 1.5%.

Projections for 2017 point to a better performance, with the global economy expected to grow by around 2.7%, thanks to an upturn in both emerging and developed economies. The emerging economies are projected to post a growth rate of 4.4% and, as in 2016, India will perform especially well, with a projected rate of 7.7% for 2017. China's growth will slow to around 6.5%. Brazil and the Russian Federation will move from negative to positive growth rates in 2017. The developed economies as a group are expected to post growth of 1.7%. Within that group, the United States will see the strongest growth, at around 1.9%, while the eurozone will exhibit a growth rate of 1.7%. Japan's economy will pick up to 0.9% growth in 2017.

Global trade volumes are growing even less than the global economy, at just 1.7% in 2106, down from 2.3% in 2015. As a result, world output growth will exceed world trade growth in the 2015-2016 biennium for the first time in 15 years, with the exception of 2009, at the height of the economic and financial crisis. The sluggish trade activity has been attributed to factors both cyclical —lacklustre global demand and a heavy fall in investment— and structural —the stalled growth in global value chains following rapid expansion in earlier periods, trends towards "localization", and the growth slowdown in China.

The global economic upturn projected for 2017, which should improve the cyclical factors mentioned, is expected to support an expansion rate in the range of 1.8% to 3.1% in the volume of global trade.

The fall in commodity prices, a very significant factor for the economies of the region, eased in 2016, with a drop of 6%, compared to 29% in 2015. These prices are expected to improve in 2017. Prices fell most heavily for energy products in 2016 (-16%), followed by minerals and metals (-4%). Agricultural products posted a slight rise in prices over the year (3%). Commodity prices are projected to rise by 8% on average in 2017, led by energy products, with a jump of 19%.

Financial market volatility eased in 2016 —with just a few short-lived spikes— and the prices of stock market assets recovered. Towards the end of the year market volatility was lower than at the January peak and stock market prices had picked up, in some cases considerably.

Consistently with these more benign international financial conditions and with changes in investors' behaviour, capital flows to emerging markets trended back upwards over the course of 2016, although remaining well below the levels seen between 2010 and 2014.

B. The external sector

The upturn in commodity prices projected for 2017 would put the region's average terms of trade back on an upward path. The fall in the region's terms of trade in 2106, at 1%, was not as steep as it had been in 2015, when they tumbled by 9%. However, the hydrocarbon-exporting countries were again the hardest hit, with an 8% fall, followed by mineral exporters (down 2%). In contrast, the Central American countries, those that export agro-industrial products, and the Caribbean (excluding Trinidad and Tobago), all benefited from lower energy prices, and their terms of trade have risen this year, albeit by less than in 2015.

For 2017, the regional terms of trade are likely to improve by about 5% on average, with a rise of around 15% for the hydrocarbon exporters, owing to an expected jump of some 20% in the oil price.

The deficit on the current account of the balance of payments narrowed from the equivalent 3.4% of GDP in 2015 to 2.2% in 2016. While the largest reduction occurred in Brazil, nearly all countries saw their current account balances improve in 2016. One of the main factors in the smaller deficit was the narrowing of the deficit on the goods account, by 81% in 2016.

External demand conditions for the region are expected to improve in 2017, and countries for which Argentina and Brazil are significant trading partners should see a recovery in intraregional trade. Economies that are more integrated with the United States could benefit from the economic upturn expected in that country in 2017, but could be hurt by the revision of trade relations following the presidential elections.

The net flow of financial resources into the region declined (by 17%) on the 2015 figure, but was more than sufficient to cover the current account deficit. As a result, the region as a whole accumulated international reserves in an amount equivalent to 0.4% of GDP.

The examination of financial flows into the region shows that the largest component was foreign direct investment (FDI), which remained broadly stable in 2016. Flows of portfolio capital and other investment net flows declined substantially in 2016, mainly because of net outflows recorded by Brazil. External bond issues by Latin American and Caribbean countries in the first 10 months of 2016 were up by 55% on the year-earlier period.

The region's sovereign risk, which peaked at 677 basis points in January 2016, retreated and was below 500 basis points in late October. As from February 2016, sovereign risk levels declined in all countries of the region, reflecting an easing of tensions on the global financial market.

C.   Economic activity

The GDP of Latin America and the Caribbean contracted by 1.1% in 2016, which translates into a 2.2% decline in per capita GDP. This negative rate of GDP growth continues the process of economic slowdown and contraction in which the region has been mired since 2011. The slowdown in the region's economic activity in 2016 was essentially due to lower growth in most of the South American economies and outright contractions in some, such as Argentina, the Bolivarian Republic of Venezuela, Brazil and Ecuador. In South America as a subregion, a contraction of 1.7% in 2015 was followed by one of 2.4% in 2016.

In Central America, growth remained strong despite a slowdown in 2016, to 3.6% from 4.7% in 2015. When Mexico is included with this group, the average falls to 2.4% for the year (compared with 3% in 2015). The economies of the English- and Dutch-speaking Caribbean contracted for the second year running (-1.7%).

The region's negative growth was caused mainly by a large drop in investment and consumption. Regionwide, domestic demand is estimated to have fallen by 2.0% in 2016, with all its components contracting: private consumption (0.9%), public consumption (1.0%) and gross fixed capital formation (6.8%). Meanwhile, imports dropped by about 3% because of weaker domestic demand, which contributed positively to output growth.

As with economic activity, in which trends contrasted between South and Central America, the behaviour of domestic demand components was also differentiated by subregion in 2016. Thus, in South America private consumption and investment both contracted (by 2.3% and 9.9%, respectively), whereas in Central America both components rose, private consumption by 3.0% and investment by 1.9%.

The Latin American and Caribbean region is expected growt 1.3% in 2017, which would put an end to the contraction of the 2015-2016 biennium. Although the upturn is projected to take place virtually across the board in 2017, as in previous years, its magnitude will vary sharply from one country to another.

D. Employment

In Latin America and the Caribbean as a whole, the quantity and quality of jobs in the labour market declined sharply during 2016. This deterioration did not take place everywhere equally, however, but was concentrated in the South American countries.

The decline in the employment rate in 2016 was accompanied by a rise in the labour market participation rate, which pushed up open unemployment. For the year and the region as a whole, the expectation is for the urban unemployment rate to have risen sharply from 7.4% in 2015 to 9.0% in 2016.

Labour market performance varied greatly across the different subregions and between men and women. In the South American countries, it is estimated that the unemployment rate rose from 8.2% in 2015 to 10.5% in 2016. By contrast, unemployment dropped from 4.9% to 4.6% in the group comprising Central America, Mexico and the Dominican Republic, and from 10.0% to 9.3% in the English-speaking Caribbean countries.

The unemployment rate rose more steeply for women, by 0.7 percentage points, in contrast with 0.3 points for the male rate, in the simple average for the countries for which information is available.

The higher unemployment rate was accompanied by a deterioration in the quality of employment, since wage-earning employment fell by 0.2% and self-employment climbed by 2.7% over the course of 2016.

Although real wages in recorded employment rose by some 1% on average in the countries with information available, this was about one percentage point less than in 2015. In the South American countries, following a very small increase in 2015, real wages held steady in the average figure. By contrast, the countries in the northern part of the region recorded a fresh increase in average real wages. The gain was somewhat smaller than in 2015, however, because nominal increases were lower and average inflation picked up slightly.

E. Policies

1. Fiscal policy

The average fiscal deficit held steady in the countries of Latin America during 2016 relative to 2015. This reflects a reduction in public spending that offset a fall in public revenues of 0.2 percentage points of GDP, so that the overall result came in at 3.0% of GDP for the second year running. The primary deficit (before interest payments) narrowed by a tenth of a percentage point to 0.8% of GDP.

Differences in individual countries' macroeconomic performance and in the economic specializations of different country groupings were reflected in a great diversity of fiscal situations in the region's economies.

Fiscal accounts have improved in the north of the region: Central America, the Dominican Republic, Haiti and Mexico. The average deficit continued to narrow in 2016, to 2.1% of GDP from -2.4% of GDP in 2015. In the case of Mexico, the federal public sector deficit also narrowed (from -3.5% to 2.9% of GDP) because of buoyant public revenues. By contrast, in other hydrocarbon-exporting countries of the region, the fiscal deficit widened.

In South America, the fiscal deficit expanded in 2016, to 3.9% of GDP from 3.6% of GDP in 2015. This reflected the fact that the drop in public revenues —which began in 2013— sharpened in 2016, when those revenues declined to 19.1% of GDP from 19.8% in 2015. The reduction in public spending as a share of GDP (from 23.4% to 23.0% of GDP) partly offset the fall in public revenues, but the fiscal deficit expanded in 2016 for the fifth year running, to 3.9% of GDP, as mentioned above.

The average fiscal deficit in the English- and Dutch-speaking Caribbean held steady at 2.5% of GDP for the second year running. Higher public spending (up from 29.9% to 30.5% of GDP) was accompanied by a similar increase in public revenues (up from 27.5% to 28.1% of GDP). The average primary result remained in surplus (0.7% of GDP), reflecting both the large share of total spending accounted for by interest payments and the commitment of governments in the subregion to reducing their high levels of public borrowing.

Gross public debt across all countries of Latin America continued its upward trend to average 37.9% of GDP in 2016, a rise of 1.3 percentage points of GDP on 2015. This trend was seen in 14 of the region's 19 countries, with Brazil having the highest public debt at 70.3% of GDP, followed by Argentina at 54.0% of GDP, Honduras at 45.9% and Uruguay at 44.8%. At the other extreme, Chile's public debt is the region's lowest at 20.6% of GDP, followed by Paraguay at 20.9% and Peru at 21.7%. The indebtedness level of a number of countries changes significantly when the net debt status is considered. In 2016, Brazil had net general government debt of 45.8% of GDP, equivalent to some 65% of its gross debt). Chile, meanwhile, had net central government debt of 3.3% of GDP and Uruguay had net debt of 20.4% of GDP, or roughly half its gross debt.

Although the level of public debt in the region increased on average in 2016, its growth slowed, because the countries opted on the whole to borrow with relative moderation and keep the public accounts sustainable by trimming public spending to offset the decline in public revenues. Conversely, the public debt burden fell in the English- and Dutch-speaking Caribbean in 2016, to 69.6% of GDP on average, a drop of 2 percentage points of GDP from 2015.

There were no substantial increases in public debt service in 2016. Only Argentina, Colombia and Honduras present increases of more than 0.5 percentage points of GDP. Interest payments in Brazil underwent a large correction in 2016, dropping by 2.2 percentage points of GDP. The cost of public debt in the Caribbean was 3.2% of GDP because of the subregion's high debt levels. Barbados and Jamaica were the countries where debt service represented the greatest cost to the fiscal accounts, at over 8% of GDP.

Reflecting fiscal consolidation, capital spending dropped by an average of 0.3 percentage points of GDP. The largest falls were in the hydrocarbon-exporting countries (Colombia, Ecuador and Trinidad and Tobago) and in Argentina, Panama and Paraguay. Conversely, public investment rose sharply in some countries of Central America (Guatemala, Honduras and Nicaragua) and in the Caribbean. Current primary spending held steady in most of the countries in 2016.

2. Monetary and exchange-rate policies and prices

In the first nine months of 2016, cumulative 12-month inflation rose in the average for the economies of Latin America and the Caribbean, from 6.9% in September 2015 to 8.4% in September 2016.[1] The rise in inflation occurred in all the subregions of Latin America and the Caribbean. In South America, the cumulative 12-month rate climbed from 9.2% in September 2015 to 10.9% in September 2016.

Cumulative 12-month inflation in the economies of the group formed by Central America, the Dominican Republic and Mexico rose, on average, from 2.5% in September 2015 to 3.4% in September 2016. In the economies of the English- and Dutch-speaking Caribbean, cumulative 12-month inflation jumped by 4.5 percentage points between September 2015 (1.8%) and September 2016 (6.3%).

As at September 2016, three economies in the region had inflation rates of over 40%: Argentina, Bolivarian Republic of Venezuela and Suriname. The economies with the lowest rates of inflation included the Bahamas, Barbados, Saint Kitts and Nevis and Saint Lucia, which reported negative rates in September 2016. In Brazil and Uruguay, inflation eased in the first nine months of 2016, although it was still above 8% in both economies.

With regard to the components of inflation, in the average for the region food prices are running ahead of the headline rate and inflation is higher in goods than in services.

During 2016, monetary and exchange-rate policies in the region were guided by different factors, chief among them the dynamics of inflation, uncertainty and thence volatility in international financial markets, and weak growth in aggregate demand.

The higher inflation observed in 2016 reduced the scope for expansionary monetary policy. Similarly, the volatility of financial markets and the repercussions for exchange rates in the region limited the potential for interest rates to be used to stimulate domestic spending. Structural differences between economies and the effects of these factors led to divergent uses being made of the different monetary policy instruments available to policymakers in the region.

In economies that use interest rates as the main instrument of monetary policy, there were differences in the frequency and direction of changes to monetary policy benchmark rates during the first 10 months of 2016. In some countries, persistently rising inflation led central banks to increase interest rates, while in others inflation fell and interest rates were used to stimulate flagging activity in the domestic economy. The differences in management of monetary policy rates have led to a situation in which these rates are at their highest for five years in economies such as Brazil, Colombia, Mexico and Peru, while in Chile, Costa Rica, the Dominican Republic, Guatemala and Paraguay they are currently close to their lowest levels since 2011.

In Latin American economies that use monetary aggregates as their main monetary policy instrument, the rate at which central banks injected money into the economy slowed in the first three quarters of 2016, reflecting trends in inflation in these economies. This meant that the nominal growth of the monetary base slackened in the South American economies (excluding the Bolivarian Republic of Venezuela), in the group formed of Central America (including only non-dollarized economies) and the Dominican Republic and in the region's dollarized economies. In the economies of the English- and Dutch-speaking Caribbean, the growth of aggregates such as the monetary base and M1 quickened slightly relative to 2015.

---

[1]   The regional and subregional averages exclude data on inflation for the Bolivarian Republic of Venezuela, since no official information is available for that country.

Lending interest rates held steady, trending slightly downward, while growth in credit to the private sector slowed.

The policies described above yielded fairly stable market interest rates, albeit with a slight downward trend in most of the region's economies. The exceptions were the economies of South America that employ the monetary policy rate as their main policy instrument, as market rates there increased slightly during 2016.

Where domestic lending is concerned, nominal growth has tended to slacken. Real-term lending growth has slowed in South America, but edged up in real terms in the group comprising Central America (including only non-dollarized economies), the Dominican Republic and Mexico, as it has in the dollarized economies.

The region's currencies tended to weaken against the dollar in a context of very volatile international financial markets, and the trend was broadly towards nominal depreciation, albeit with great volatility over the year.

In the comparison between the values for December 2015 and November 2016, the currencies of 13 countries in the region depreciated against the dollar in nominal terms. The five countries with the largest depreciations, all of them by over 15%, were Argentina, Bolivarian Republic of Venezuela, Haiti, Mexico and Suriname. A number of the region's currencies have shown a tendency to appreciate in the second half of 2016, which has lessened the average depreciation over the first 11 months of the year.

International reserves increased slightly (by 2.1%) in the first 11 months of 2016 relative to the end of 2015. However, they remained below their 2014 level. Reserves increased in 22 of the region's economies, with the largest rises being in Ecuador (61.6%), Argentina (46.9%), Dominica and El Salvador (25.0%) and Saint Kitts and Nevis (22.3%). Meanwhile, reserves contracted in 10 countries, most notably the Bolivarian Republic of Venezuela (28.2%), the Plurinational State of Bolivia (20.3%), Belize (14.7%) and Uruguay (11.7%). Among the economies with the highest levels of international reserves, particular mention should be made of increases in Brazil and Chile, amounting to 2.6% and 2.1%, respectively.

The conjunction of a larger build-up of nominal reserves and low economic growth has pushed up the ratio of international reserves to GDP in the region as a whole, so that this indicator rose for the fourth year running, to 17.7% of GDP.

F.   Risks and outlook for 2017

Global risks and uncertainties in 2107 will have diverse effects on the region's economic performance. Sluggish growth of the global economy, which has now lasted for over a decade, with average growth of 2.5% in the period 2013-2016, will continue: the average projected for 2017-2018 is 2.8%. This slack performance has been accompanied by slowing productivity —which shows a growth rate of around 1%— and declining rates of growth in global investment and trade. The positive effects of an upturn in 2017 for global trade, which should grow by between 1.8% and 3.1%, could be overshadowed by the mounting protectionism seen since the United Kingdom voted to leave the European Union (Brexit).

In financial markets, the expected normalization of interest rates could increase uncertainly and financial volatility, given the dynamics of financial asset prices. Although the likelihood remains that interest rate rises will be gradual, this could still affect financial flows to emerging markets, including those of Latin America and the Caribbean. Concerns also persist over the financial stability of economies in which credit, especially in the form of international bond issues, has grown strongly, since these could be hurt by higher interest rates on dollar liabilities. This is in addition to concerns over the position of a number of financial institutions in developed countries, chiefly in the eurozone.

To these complex financial and economic growth dynamics have been added uncertainties that could have major impacts on economic performance in the coming years. Recent protectionist trends have raised new uncertainties and risks regarding the future of the global economy. These trends reflect the mounting tensions and difficulties in reconciling and coordinating national policy emphases and aims with the institutional arrangements governing international movements of goods and services, finance and capital, technology and migration in a globalized world.

In this context, global trade —following the questioning of free trade agreements such as the Trans-Pacific Partnership (TPP) and the North American Free Trade Agreement (NAFTA)— is not the only area of tension. The value chain dynamics of global manufacturing, as well as technology mobility, will also be affected. Multilateralism could well be weakened by a stronger tendency towards bilateral agreements on trade and investment.

As in preceding years, global economic conditions will have different effects on the various countries and subregions of Latin America and the Caribbean, and will sharpen subregional differences by the production and trade orientation of their economies.

Although the protectionist tendencies emerging in the United States will have global and regional effects, the possible renegotiation of NAFTA and other trade agreements, as well as uncertainty over the dynamics of monetary transfers from migrants, will have significant effects in particular on Mexico and Central America, which export most of their manufactures and services to the United States. The performance of the economies in the south of the region should benefit from the projected upturn in their terms of trade, although uncertainty remains over the economic future of the eurozone and China.

Terms of trade are expected to improve in the average for Latin America and the Caribbean in 2017, along with an upturn in extraregional demand and a recovery of intraregional trade, thanks to a stronger performance by the economies of the southern part of the region, especially Argentina and Brazil.

Domestic demand in the countries of the region slowed heavily in 2016, mainly owing to a heavy drop in investment and consumption by both public and private sectors. These trends should improve in 2017.

Regaining a growth path will require reversing these trends, with an emphasis on investment, which in turn will require strong mobilization of financial resources. The growing difficulties faced by the countries of the region in financing countercyclical fiscal policy, added to their status as middle-income countries —which hinders their access to external concessional financing and to international cooperation funding—, mean that mobilizing domestic and external resources to finance investment must be a policy priority for the countries in the near term.

To regain fiscal space, it is essential to reduce tax evasion and avoidance, which are very significant in the region. The Economic Commission or Latin America and the Caribbean (ECLAC) estimates that tax evasion and avoidance cost the region the equivalent of 2.4 percentage points of GDP in the case of VAT and 4.3 percentage points in the case of income tax. This represented a total of US$ 340 billion in 2015, or 6.7% of regional GDP. Budget adjustments involving cuts in public investment could deepen the recessionary conditions, because this investment, like private investment, plays a key role in short- and long-run growth. Estimates show that fiscal multipliers are high and significant in the region, and that the public investment multiplier exceeds 2 after two years.

Unlike in 2016 when the region contracted by 1.1%, and despite complex external conditions and a number of risks, the region's economy is expected to switch direction and return positive growth of 1.3%. As in 2016, the weighted average growth figure masks different growth dynamics between countries and subregions. Central America, including the Spanish-speaking Caribbean and Haiti, is expected to grow by around 3.7% in 2017; including Mexico, with a projected growth rate of 1.9%, brings the average down to 2.3%. Positive growth is projected in 2017 for South America, at 0.9%, and for the English-speaking Caribbean, at 1.3%.

Global economic trends

The global economy grew by 2.2% in 2016, the lowest rate since the international financial crisis of 2008-2009, and growth is expected to pick up slightly to 2.7% in 2017

Although global trade volume continued to slow in 2016 —with just 1.7% growth over the year— the World Trade Organization (WTO) expects this to recover in 2017, with expansion of between 1.8% and 3.1%

Prices for primary products bottomed out in January 2016, and have begun to rise again since then; overall they are expected to show a drop of 6% for 2016, and a recovery of 8% in 2017

Financial market volatility eased in 2016 —notwithstanding a few short-lived spikes— and the prices of stock market assets have recovered

The global economy grew by 2.2% in 2016, the lowest rate since the international financial crisis of 2008-2009, and growth is expected to pick up slightly to 2.7% in 2017

With respect to the previous year, world economic growth slowed 0.3 percentage points in 2016, to 2.2%, the lowest rate since the international financial crisis of 2008-2009. A lower growth rate had not occurred since 2002.

The developed economies as a group expanded by 1.5%, compared with a rate of 3.6% for the developing countries. This represented a slowdown for both groups, which had posted rates of 2.1% and 3.8% respectively, in 2015.

Projections for 2017 point to a slightly better global growth performance (2.7%), thanks to an upturn in the group of emerging economies, and a slight improvement in the group of developed economies (see figure I.1).

Figure I.1
Selected regions and countries: gross domestic product growth, 2013-2017[a]
(Percentages)

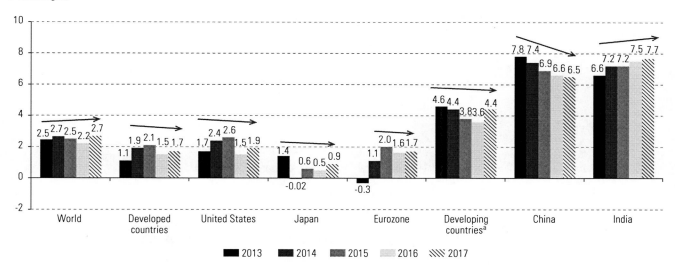

Source: Economic Commission for Latin America and the Caribbean (ECLAC), on the basis of United Nations, *World Economic Situation and Prospects*, 2015, 2016, 2017 and International Monetary Fund (IMF), *World Economic Outlook (WEO). Subdued Demand: Symptoms and Remedies*, October 2016.

[a] The figures for 2016 are estimates and those for 2017 are projections, both from *World Economic Situation and Prospects, 2017*.

India will continue to post the fastest GDP growth among the large emerging economies, with a projected rate of 7.7% for 2017. China's growth, while forecast to slow to 6.5% in 2017, remains much stronger than that of other large economies, such as Brazil and the Russian Federation, whose output contracted in 2016 (by 3.6% and 0.9%, respectively), but should return to growth in 2017 (0.5% and 0.8%, respectively). For the group of emerging economies overall, then, growth will pick up by around 0.8 percentage points to 4.4% in 2017.

The developed economies as a group are expected to post growth of 1.7% in 2017, a slight upturn over 2016. Within that group, the United States will see growth strengthen (0.4 percentage points with respect to 2016) to 1.9%, while the eurozone will register slightly stronger growth than in 2016 (1.7%). Japan's economy will pick up to 0.9% growth which, although still very low, is higher than the average for 2014-2016 (0.4%).

Although global trade volume continued to slow in 2016 —with just 1.7% growth over the year— the World Trade Organization (WTO) expects this to recover in 2017, with expansion of between 1.8% and 3.1%

The volume of global trade will continue to slacken in 2016. Trade was growing at annual rates of 8% on average before the global crisis of 2008-2009, but since then has expanded very little (see figure I.2). For 2016 overall, WTO projects growth of 1.7% in trade volumes, a lower rate than in 2015 (2.3%) and the lowest since the global crisis of 2008-2009.

Figure I.2
World: year-on-year variation in trade volume, three-month rolling averages, 2003-2016
(Percentages)

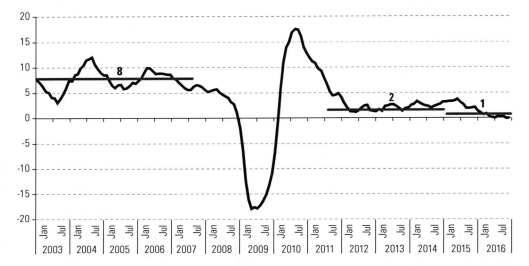

Source: Economic Commission for Latin America and the Caribbean (ECLAC), on the basis of figures from the Netherlands Bureau of Economic Policy Analysis (CPB).

The slack trade rendering reflects a disappointing import performance across all the subregions (see figure I.3).

Figure I.3
Year-on-year variation in import volumes, three-month rolling averages, December 2014 to August 2016
(Percentages)

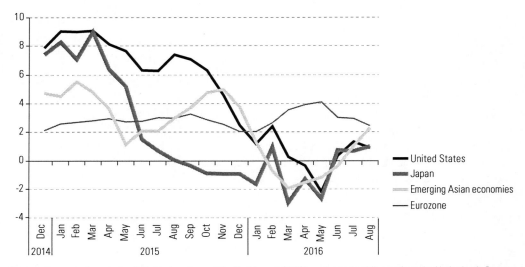

Source: Economic Commission for Latin America and the Caribbean (ECLAC), on the basis of figures from the Netherlands Bureau of Economic Policy Analysis (CPB).

Global trade has slowed so heavily that world output growth will exceed world trade growth in the 2015-2016 biennium. Historically, the opposite is more normal, with world trade usually expanding between 1.5 and 2 times faster than global GDP (see figure I.4).[1]

Figure I.4
Annual variation in global trade volume and in global GDP, average by subperiod, 1981-2016
(Percentages)

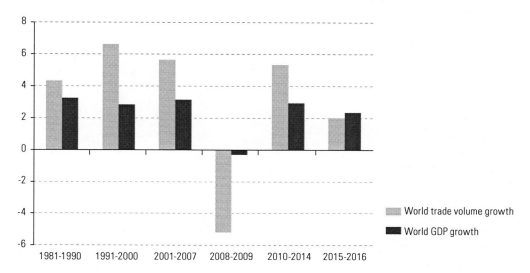

Source: Economic Commission for Latin America and the Caribbean (ECLAC), on the basis of World Trade Organization (WTO) figures and International Monetary Fund (IMF), World Economic Outlook Database, October 2016.

The sluggish goods trade has been attributed to both cyclical and structural factors. Among the former are lacklustre demand since the international financial crisis, slack investment —since investment is a demand component that is trade-intensive— and weak economic activity in the eurozone, a trade-intensive region. The structural factors include the stalled growth in global value chains following rapid expansion in earlier periods, a tendency by transnational corporations to seek local suppliers of inputs (localization), and the growth slowdown in China owing to its structural transformation from an export-driven economy to a consumption- and service-based model.[2]

However, given that lower demand and —especially— lower investment are the strongest forces weakening trade,[3] the upturn in global economy activity projected for 2017 should halt the deceleration of trade volumes. In its September 2016 report, in fact, WTO stated that it expected global trade to grow between 1.8% and 3.1% in 2017.

Nevertheless, global trade —owing to the questioning of free trade agreements such as the Trans-Pacific Partnership (TPP) and the North American Free Trade Agreement (NAFTA)— is subject to tensions. The value chain dynamics of global manufacturing, as well as technology mobility, will also be affected. Multilateralism could well be weakened by a stronger tendency towards bilateral agreements on trade and investment.

---

[1] See World trade Organization (WTO), "Trade statistics and outlook. Trade in 2016 to grow at slowest pace since the financial crisis", *Press Release*, No. 779, 27 September 2016 [online] https://www.wto.org/english/news_e/pres16_e/pr779_e.pdf.

[2] See United Nations, *World Economic Situation and Prospects,* 2017 and International Monetary Fund (IMF), *World Economic Outlook (WEO). Subdued Demand: Symptoms and Remedies*, October 2016.

[3] IMF attributes about three quarters of the decline in global import growth between the pre- and post-crisis periods (between 2003-2007 and 2012-2015) to lower levels of demand and investment.

Prices for primary products bottomed out in January 2016, and have begun to rise again since then; overall they are expected to show a drop of 6% for 2016, and a recovery of 8% in 2017

The contraction in prices in 2016 was not nearly as severe as in 2015 (6%, compared with 29%).[4] As in 2015, the category of energy products (oil, gas natural and coal) showed the heaviest fall in 2016 (-16%), followed by minerals and metals (-4%). Agricultural products posted a slight rise in prices over the year (3%) (see table I.1).

Table I.1
Annual variation in international prices for primary products, 2015, 2016 and 2017[a]
(Percentages)

	2015	2016	2017
Agricultural and livestock products	-16	3	2
Foods, tropical beverages and oilseeds	-18	4	2
Foods	-15	8	2
Tropical beverages	-21	-1	5
Oils and oilseeds	-22	0	2
Forestry and agricultural raw materials	-6	-1	0
Minerals and metals	-23	-4	3
Energy	-42	-16	19
Crude oil	-47	-16	20
Total for primary products	**-29**	**-6**	**8**
Total for primary products (excluding energy)	**-19**	**-0.2**	**2**

Source: Economic Commission for Latin America and the Caribbean (ECLAC), on the basis of figures provided by Bloomberg, the World Bank, the International Monetary Fund (IMF) and The Economist Intelligence Unit.
[a] The figures for 2016 are estimates and those for 2017 are projections.

Commodity prices are projected to rise by 8% on average in 2017 which, as will be discussed in chapter II, will improve the terms of trade for commodity-exporting countries. The projections of specialized agencies indicate that energy products will post the strongest recovery in 2017, at 19%, while other commodities will see prices edge up by 2%.

Oil prices are expected to trend back up again in 2017 after their 58% fall between mid-2014 and November 2016. Although oil inventories have remained high throughout 2016, production cuts announced by the Organization of the Petroleum Exporting Countries (OPEC) have led to higher price projections for crude oil. Although global demand for crude oil is expected to edge up (1%), driven mainly by the emerging economies (2.3%) given that demand in the developed economies will remain flat, supply by non-OPEC producers will increase little in 2017 (0.6%). However, the current oil prices are in line with the average for the last 50 years, so the effects of OPEC capacity to limit supply remain to be seen.[5]

Prices of mining products will likely rise by 3%, according to the latest projection revisions, owing to production restrictions for some of them, such as zinc, lead and tin.

Favourable supply conditions for most agricultural products account for the modest price rise projected, of 2% for the group overall. However, agricultural price trends are subject to ever-present climate risks, and some impact may be expected from the protectionist measures implemented by economies such as India or from changes in inventory management policy by China.

---

[4]   These indices are calculated on the basis of products weighted by their relative share in the export basket of the Latin American and Caribbean countries.
[5]   See Organization of the Petroleum Exporting Countries (OPEC), *Monthly Oil Market Report OPEC, 12 October 2016* [online] http://www.opec.org/opec_web/static_files_project/media/downloads/publications/MOMR%20October%202016.pdf.

Financial market volatility eased in 2016 —notwithstanding a few short-lived spikes— and the prices of stock market assets have recovered

Towards the end of the year market volatility was lower than at the January peak and stock market prices had recovered, in some cases considerably (see figures I.5 and I.6). Consistently with these more benign international financial conditions and with changes in investors' appetite for risk, capital flows to emerging markets have been trending back upwards over the course of 2016, but they remain well below the levels seen between 2010 and 2014 (see figure I.7).

Figure I.5
Implied market volatility indices,[a] January 2015 to November 2016

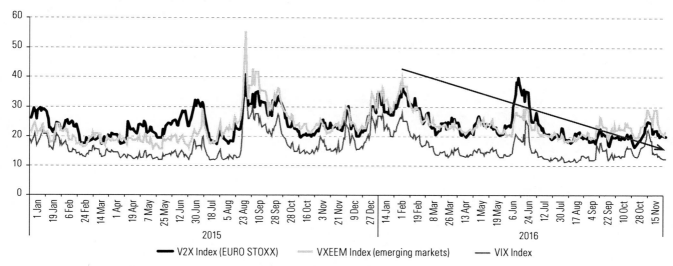

Source: Economic Commission for Latin America and the Caribbean (ECLAC), on the basis of Bloomberg.
Note: The VIX Index is prepared by the Chicago Board Options Exchange (CBOE) from S&P 500 call and put option prices, and measures expected volatility over the next 30 days. Following the same logic, the CBOE also produces the VXEEM index, which measures volatility in emerging markets, while Deutsche Börse and Goldman Sachs produce the V2X index, which measures eurozone volatility.

Figure I.6
Stock market indices (MSCI)[a]
(Index: 1 January 2016-100)

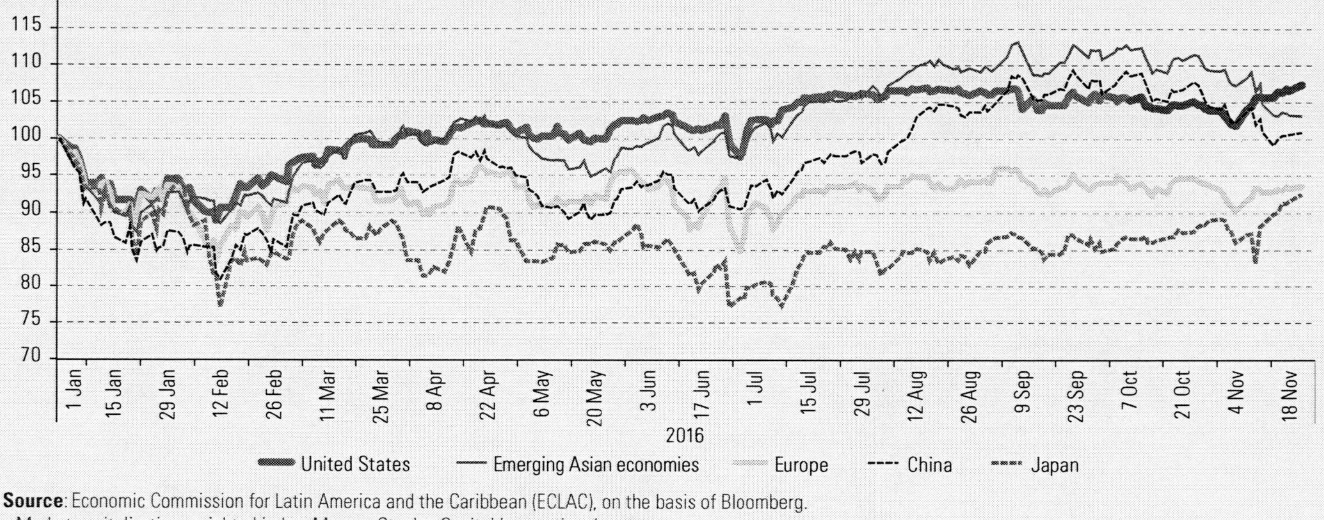

Source: Economic Commission for Latin America and the Caribbean (ECLAC), on the basis of Bloomberg.
[a] Market capitalization weighted index, Morgan Stanley Capital International.

Figure I.7

12-month cumulative portfolio capital flows to emerging markets, January 2006 to October 2016[a]

(Billions of dollars)

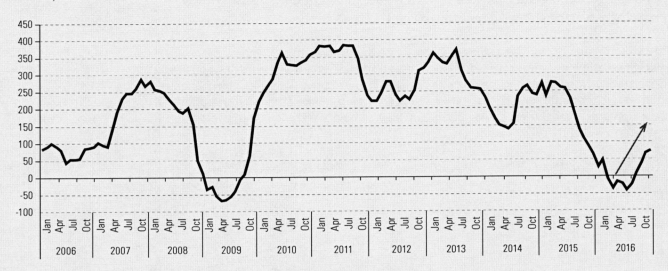

Source: Economic Commission for Latin America and the Caribbean (ECLAC), on the basis of Bloomberg.

[a] Monthly indicator of portfolio capital flows prepared by the Institute of International Finance (IIF).

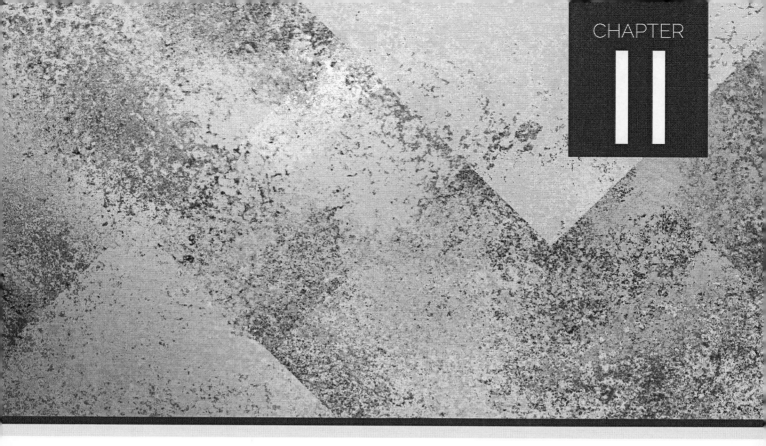

The external sector

In 2016, the terms of trade fell by much less than in 2015, although hydrocarbon exporters are still facing substantially lower export prices

The balance-of-payments current account deficit narrowed sharply in 2016, mainly owing to a reduction in the deficit on the goods account, although all components of the current account contributed

The reduction in goods imports has generated a significant improvement in the goods balance in 2016

The net financial flows received by Latin America in 2016 were 17% smaller than in 2015; but they were more than sufficient to cover the current account deficit, so the region as a whole accumulated international reserves

External bond issues by Latin American and Caribbean countries in the first 10 months of 2016 are up by 55% on the year-earlier period

The region's sovereign risk, which peaked at 677 basis points in January 2016, retreated and was below 500 basis points in late October

The region's current account deficit narrowed sharply in 2016, mainly owing to the fall in import values associated with weak economic growth. Although net financial inflows were smaller than in 2015, they were more than sufficient to cover the deficit; and the region built up international reserves during the year. Sovereign risk has declined everywhere in the region since February, reflecting an easing of tensions on global financial markets and a simultaneous increase in international bond issues by individual countries.

In 2016, the terms of trade fell by much less than in 2015, although hydrocarbon exporters are still facing substantially lower export prices

In line with the global trend of commodity prices, the regional terms of trade fell by 1% in 2016, much less than the 9% drop recorded in the previous year. Hydrocarbon-exporting countries have again been hit hardest, with a 8% fall, followed by mineral exporters, for which the terms of trade declined by 2%. In contrast, the Central American countries, those that export agro-industrial products, and the Caribbean (excluding Trinidad and Tobago), have all benefited from lower energy prices; and their terms of trade have risen this year, albeit by less than in 2015 (see figure II.1).

Figure II.1
Latin America and the Caribbean (selected countries and country groupings): rate of variation in the terms of trade, 2013-2017[a]
(Percentages)

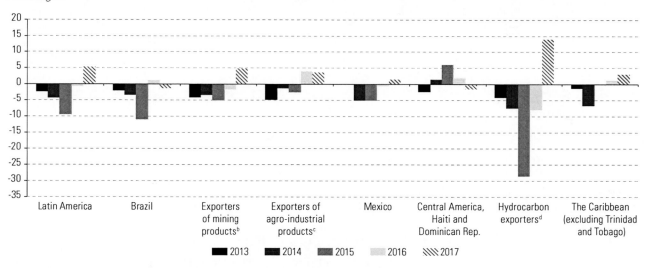

Source: Economic Commission for Latin America and the Caribbean (ECLAC), on the basis of official figures.
[a] The figures for 2016 and 2017 are estimations and projections, respectively.
[b] Chile and Peru.
[c] Argentina, Paraguay and Uruguay.
[d] Bolivarian Republic of Venezuela, Colombia, Ecuador, Trinidad and Tobago and Plurinational State of Bolivia.

For 2017, if commodity prices recover as projected, the regional terms of trade are likely to improve, by about 5% on average; although the effects on individual countries will depend on the weight of commodities in their export and import baskets. In this case, the hydrocarbon exporters are likely to benefit most, with their terms of trade set to improve by about 15%, since oil is forecast to post the strongest percentage price recovery in 2017 (by around 20%), having suffered the steepest falls in the previous two years.

The balance-of-payments current account deficit narrowed sharply in 2016, mainly owing to a reduction in the deficit on the goods account, although all components of the current account contributed

The deficit on the current account of the balance of payments was equivalent to 2.2% of regional gross domestic product (GDP) (US$ 104.8 billion) in 2016, compared to 3.4% of GDP (US$ 175.2 billion) a year earlier (see figure II.2). While the largest reduction occurred in Brazil, nearly all countries saw their current account balances improve in 2016.[1]

For the region as a whole, all components of the current account helped to reduce the deficit, although the goods account was the main contributor, with the shortfall shrinking by 81% in 2016 (from US$ 52.9 billion in 2015 to US$ 9.8 billion in 2016).[2]

Figure II.2
Latin America: balance-of-payments current account by component, 2005-2016[a]
(Percentages of GDP)

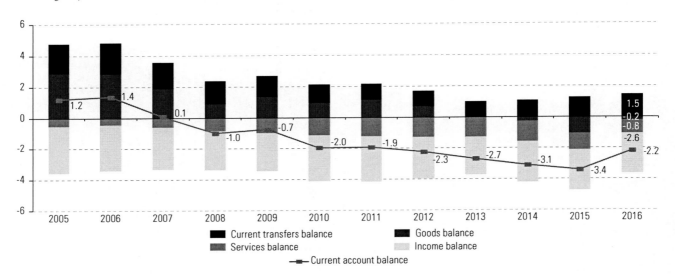

Legend:
- Current transfers balance
- Services balance
- Goods balance
- Income balance
- Current account balance

Source: Economic Commission for Latin America and the Caribbean (ECLAC), on the basis of official figures.
[a] The figures for 2016 are projections.

The reduction in goods imports has generated a significant improvement in the goods balance in 2016

The goods account deficit has narrowed sharply in 2016, owing to a 9% fall in the value of imports relative to the previous year's level, which more than offset the 5% drop in goods exports.

The region's lacklustre economic activity has drawn in smaller import volumes (-4%), which, combined with lower prices (-5%), has produced the reduction in import value noted above. Recessions in some of the region's main economies, such as Argentina, Brazil and Ecuador and, have also reduced imports substantially, by some 6%, 24% and 19%, respectively (see figure II.3).

[1] Excluding Brazil, the current account deficit in 2016 is 2.7%, compared to 3.5% in 2015.
[2] If Brazil is excluded, there is still a reduction in the trade deficit, but only by 24%.

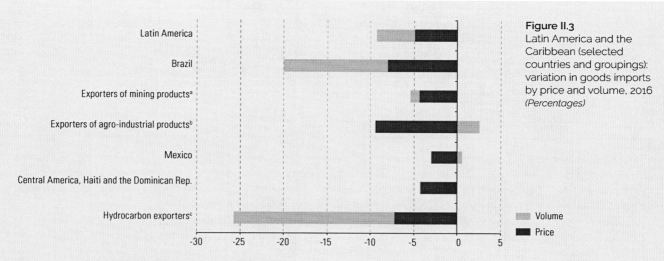

Figure II.3
Latin America and the Caribbean (selected countries and groupings): variation in goods imports by price and volume, 2016
(Percentages)

Source: Economic Commission for Latin America and the Caribbean (ECLAC).
ᵃ Chile and Peru.
ᵇ Argentina, Paraguay and Uruguay.
ᶜ Bolivarian Republic of Venezuela, Colombia, Ecuador, Trinidad and Tobago and Plurinational State of Bolivia.

The region has seen declining exports for the fourth straight year, as a result of lower export prices (down by more than 5%), despite volumes growing by 1% (see figure II.4). In 2016, exports have declined in all country groupings.

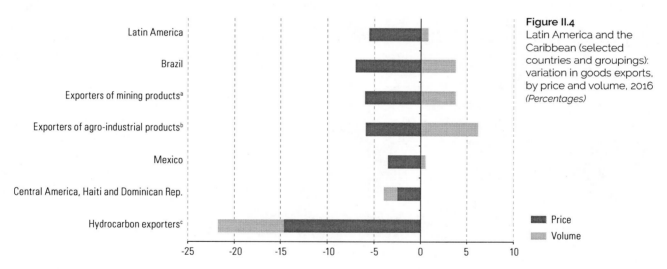

Figure II.4
Latin America and the Caribbean (selected countries and groupings): variation in goods exports, by price and volume, 2016
(Percentages)

Source: Economic Commission for Latin America and the Caribbean (ECLAC).
ᵃ Chile and Peru.
ᵇ Argentina, Paraguay and Uruguay.
ᶜ Bolivarian Republic of Venezuela, Colombia, Ecuador, Trinidad and Tobago and Plurinational State of Bolivia.

Countries whose exports are based on hydrocarbons, such as the Bolivarian Republic of Venezuela, Colombia, Ecuador, the Plurinational State of Bolivia, and Trinidad and Tobago, are reporting falls of around 21% largely as a result of lower prices (-15%) but also of smaller export volumes (-7%). In Chile and Peru, which export mainly mining products, lower prices (-6%) were partly offset by larger volumes (up 4%), and this helped cushion the 2% fall in value exported. Countries that export agro-industrial products, such as Argentina, Paraguay and Uruguay, have also compensated for lower export prices (-6%) with volume growth (6%), and in these cases export value has held up. In the case of Brazil, the larger volumes exported (4%) were insufficient to offset the 7% fall in their prices, which resulted in exports shrinking by 4% in 2016. In Central America, exports are down by about 4% in 2016, and Mexico's foreign sales shrank by 3%; in the latter case, however, the falling oil price had a significant impact.

Similarly to 2015, in terms of export destinations, intraregional sales accounted for most of the fall in 2016 (see box II.1).

Box II.1
Contribution of each destination to the reduction in goods exports

In 2016 the value of goods exports from Latin America has fallen by nearly 5%, chiefly owing to reduced sales to the United States (which explains 1.8 percentage points of the total fall) and within the Latin America and the Caribbean region (1.6 percentage points of the fall). These two destinations had also been the main causes of the 15% decrease in exports in 2015, with the United States accounting for 3 percentage points and Latin America and the Caribbean nearly 4 points.

The fact that the drop in export value is largely explained by a reduction in intraregional exports since 2014, has meant that the intraregional trade coefficient has been declining significantly since then.[a] While this indicator maintained levels around 20% from mid-2007 until late 2013, it ended the current year at just 15%, its lowest value since 2002.

South America is the subregion hit hardest by the reduction in intraregional exports; of a total fall of 6.4% in export value in 2016, nearly 3 percentage points are explained by weaker sales within the region, while exports to the United States generate a smaller relative impact (around 1 percentage point), and the European Union also accounts for nearly 1 percentage point. Exports to China and the rest of Asia jointly explain only half of a percentage point of the reduction in exports.

It has generally been argued that the downward trend in intraregional trade could restrict the region's potential to diversify exports and increase its productivity, since Latin America is the main recipient of the region's own manufactures —and hence of higher value added exports.[b] Nonetheless, an encouraging sign in this regard is that in South America the sharp fall in exports to the region is closely related to recessionary processes in some of the leading economies of the subregion during this year (Argentina, Brazil, Ecuador and the Bolivarian Republic of Venezuela), so the trend can be expected to reverse given the positive 2017 growth forecasts for the first three economies mentioned.[c]

Exports from Central America and Mexico are down by 2.8% overall in 2016, including a reduction of nearly 2 percentage points in sales to their leading market and northern neighbour, the United States. In fact, the latter has been cutting its import volumes sharply since early 2015, and this has had more of an impact on the subregion than the fall in intraregional exports of just over one half a percentage point.

Latin America: contribution of each destination to the fall in goods exports, 2016
(Percentages)

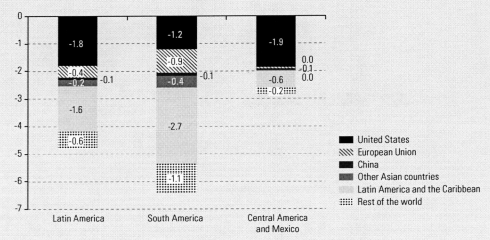

Source: Economic Commission for Latin America and the Caribbean (ECLAC).
Note: Projections on the basis of data for January-July. Central America includes Costa Rica, El Salvador, Guatemala, Honduras and Nicaragua.

Source: Economic Commission for Latin America and the Caribbean (ECLAC).
[a] The intraregional trade coefficient is defined as the intraregional share in total exports (or imports).
[b] ECLAC, *Latin America and the Caribbean in the World Economy, 2016. Briefing paper* [online] http://repositorio.cepal.org/bitstream/handle/11362/40745/1/S1600895_en.pdf.
[c] Another factor influencing the decline in intraregional exports has been the fall in energy prices, for example in Ecuador and in the Plurinational State of Bolivia (see ECLAC, ibid).

The shortfall on the income account —where outgoing payments associated with foreign direct investment (FDI) and interest on the external debt generate a structural deficit— narrowed from US$ 131.8 billion in 2015 to US$ 124.3 billion, mainly as a result of smaller profit repatriations by transnational enterprises, which continued to face lower export prices.

The current transfers account posted a surplus again, with the 2016 figure (US$ 69.2 billion) higher than in the previous year (US$ 65.1). The main component of this account is migrant remittances flowing into the countries of the region, which, according to the October figures, were up by an average of 7% year-on-year (see figure II.5).

Figure II.5
Latin America and the Caribbean (selected countries): variation in migrant remittance inflows, 2014-2016[a]
(Percentages)

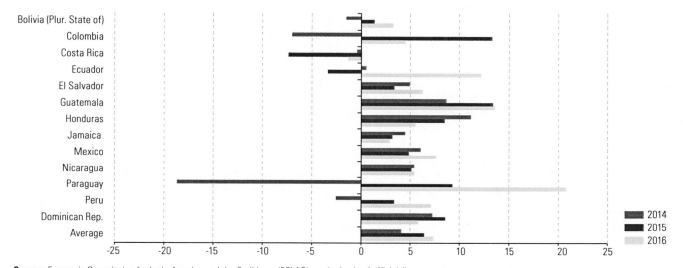

Source: Economic Commission for Latin America and the Caribbean (ECLAC), on the basis of official figures.
[a] The figures for 2016 correspond to January-October in the cases of Colombia, Guatemala, El Salvador and the Dominican Republic; January-September for Honduras, Mexico and Paraguay; January-August in the cases of Brazil and the Plurinational State of Bolivia; and January-June for Costa Rica, Ecuador, Jamaica and Peru.

Looking ahead, if the projections for the recovery of economic activity and world trade are borne out in 2017, the region's external demand could also pick up.

The weighted average rate of GDP growth of the trade partners of the region's countries is forecast to be higher than in 2016 in all cases. In the case of Chile, for example, although the country's main trading partner, China, is expected to see slower economic growth in the coming year, the other countries with which Chile trades could more than take up the slack; so its trade partners' weighted growth rate should be somewhat higher (see table II.1).

Intraregional trade is also expected to recover in 2017 for countries that trade intensively with Argentina and Brazil (such as Paraguay and Uruguay), given the relatively stronger economic activity projected for these countries in the coming year.

The economies that trade more heavily with United States are likely to benefit from the greater vibrancy projected for the country's economy in 2017, but they could also be hurt by the revision of trade agreements. The United States is currently the largest export market for Colombia (28% of the country's total goods exports), Costa Rica (41%), Ecuador (39%), El Salvador (47%), Guatemala (36%), Honduras (44%), Jamaica (39%), Mexico (81%), Nicaragua (54%) and Panama (20%); so trade flows in these countries could be affected to some extent for these reasons.

Table II.1
Latin America: indicator of the growth of trading partners, 2015-2017[a]
(Percentages)

	2015	2016	2017
South America			
Argentina	1.7	1.6	2.6
Bolivia (Plurinational State of)	0.7	0.2	1.9
Brazil	3.0	2.7	3.1
Chile	3.1	2.9	3.2
Colombia	2.3	2.0	2.3
Ecuador	2.4	2.3	2.7
Peru	3.0	2.7	2.9
Paraguay	-0.1	-0.2	1.7
Uruguay	1.2	1.1	2.0
Venezuela (Bolivarian Republic of)	4.0	3.9	4.0
Central America and Mexico			
Costa Rica	2.8	2.7	2.8
Dominican Republic	1.9	2.1	2.4
El Salvador	3.1	3.1	3.1
Guatemala	2.7	2.7	2.9
Honduras	2.5	2.4	2.6
Mexico	2.4	2.3	2.5
Nicaragua	2.1	1.9	2.2
Panama	2.7	2.6	2.7

Source: Economic Commission for Latin America and the Caribbean (ECLAC), on the basis of information from the United Nations Commodity Trade Database (COMTRADE), for trade partner weightings, and International Monetary Fund (IMF) World Economic Outlook, October 2016, for GDP growth projections.

[a] The growth rates have been weighted by each partner's share in the total goods exports of the Latin American country in question.

In addition to external demand factors, another influence on trade values in 2017 will be commodity prices, which are projected to be 8% higher on average than in 2016. This heralds a stronger export performance by economies that are specialized in exporting these products, mainly those of South America.

The net financial flows received by Latin America in 2016 were 17% smaller than in 2015; but they were more than sufficient to cover the current account deficit, so the region as a whole accumulated international reserves

In 2016, the net flow of financial resources into the region (in other words the balance-of-payments capital and financial account),[3] amounted to 2.6% of GDP, which was more than sufficient to cover the current account deficit (-2.2% of GDP). As a result, the region as a whole accumulated international reserves in an amount equivalent to 0.4% of GDP (an increase of more than 2% in the reserves stock).

Although total flows into the region in 2016 were 17% down on the previous year's level, this mainly reflects the reduction in Brazil, since flows to the rest of the economies increased by 8% on average.

---

[3] The capital and financial account balance includes balance-of-payments errors and omissions.

The financial account reveals differentiated patterns between net FDI, on the one hand, and portfolio capital (essentially investments in bonds and shares) and net other investment flows (mostly cross-border deposits and loans), on the other.

FDI is the main financial inflow to the region as a whole, representing around US$ 133.5 billion in 2015, and remaining broadly stable in 2016 (see figure II.6).[4]

Meanwhile, the other financial account items (portfolio capital and net other investment flows) declined substantially in 2016, mainly because Brazil recorded net outflows in this category in the first three quarters of 2016.

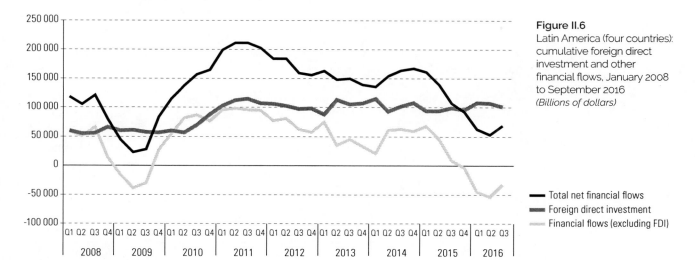

Figure II.6
Latin America (four countries): cumulative foreign direct investment and other financial flows, January 2008 to September 2016
(Billions of dollars)

— Total net financial flows
▬ Foreign direct investment
— Financial flows (excluding FDI)

Source: Economic Commission for Latin America and the Caribbean (ECLAC), on the basis of official figures.

External bond issues by Latin American and Caribbean countries in the first 10 months of 2016 are up by 55% on the year-earlier period

A significant part of the increase in debt issuances reflected the Argentine sovereign sector's return to the markets following the agreement with the debt-restructuring holdouts and new issuances by the Brazilian State oil company (Petrobras), although other countries in the region increased their issuances as well.

Mexico issued the largest volume of debt in absolute terms in 2016 —over 20% more than in 2015. The second largest issuer was Argentina, where, in addition to the sovereign sector, corporate issues increased eightfold year-on-year in January-October 2016; and the quasi-sovereign sector, mainly the provinces, tripled their issues.

The cumulative volume of bond issues over the last 12 months reflects an upturn in all sectors, although the supranational institutions lead the issuance growth rates, along with sovereigns and quasi-sovereigns (see figure II.7 and table II.2).[5]

---

[4]   Financial-account data is available up to the third quarter of 2016 for four countries whose FDI flows represented 72% of the regional total in 2015.

[5]   The quasi-sovereign sector includes public-sector development banks and State-owned enterprises, among other entities. The supranational sector includes regional development banks, such as the Development Bank of Latin American (CAF) and the Central American Bank for Economic Integration (CABEI).

Figure II.7
Latin America and the Caribbean: annual variation in cumulative debt issues on international markets over the last 12 months by institutional sector, January 2009-October 2016
(Billions of dollars)

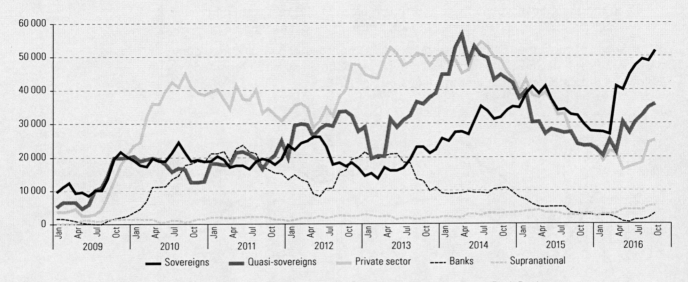

Source: Economic Commission for Latin America and the Caribbean (ECLAC), on the basis of figures from the Latin Finance Bonds Database.

Table II.2
Latin America and the Caribbean: variation in debt issues on international markets by institutional sector, 2015-2016[a]
(Percentages)

Institutional sector	Variation
Supranational	102
Sovereigns	87
Quasi-sovereigns	55
Banks	14
Private sector	10
Total	55

Source: Economic Commission for Latin America and the Caribbean (ECLAC), on the basis of figures from the Latin Finance Bonds.
[a] Refers to the period January-October for each year.

The region's sovereign risk, which peaked at 677 basis points in January 2016, retreated and was below 500 basis points in late October

As from February this year, sovereign risk levels declined in all countries of the region, reflecting an easing of tensions on the global financial market.

Between the peak in January and late October 2016, the regional Emerging Market Bond Index Global (EMBIG) fell by 210 basis points, chiefly as sovereign risk decreased in countries that had suffered sharp rises in 2015, such as the Bolivarian Republic of Venezuela, Brazil, and Ecuador (see figure II.8).[6] The regional index stood at 467 basis points in late October 2016; and the countries with the highest sovereign risk levels are Bolivarian Republic of Venezuela (2,316 basis points) and Ecuador (743 basis points) (see table II.3).

---

[6]   Sovereign risk in the Bolivarian Republic of Venezuela was improved by a debt swap undertaken by the oil company Petróleos de Venezuela (PDVSA).

Figure II.8
Latin America (13 countries): sovereign risk according to the Emerging Markets Bond Index Global (EMBIG), January 2012 to October 2016
(Basis points)

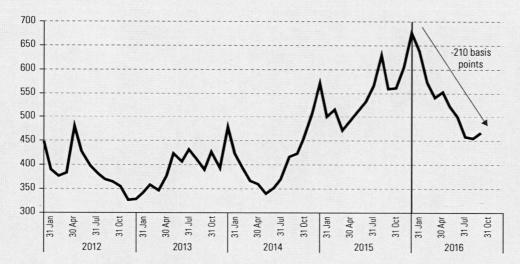

Source: Economic Commission for Latin America and the Caribbean (ECLAC), on the basis of figures from JP Morgan.

Country	31 December 2015	29 January 2016	31 October 2016
Argentina	438	502	452
Bolivia (Plurinational State of)	250	262	130
Brazil	548	540	316
Chile	253	274	177
Colombia	317	378	237
Dominican Republic	421	498	386
Ecuador	1 266	1 509	743
Mexico	315	362	293
Panama	214	246	168
Paraguay	338	364	268
Peru	240	273	155
Uruguay	280	317	230
Venezuela (Bolivarian Republic of)	2 807	3 560	2 316
Latin America	**605**	**677**	**467**

Table II.3
Latin America (13 countries): Emerging Markets Bond Index Global (EMBIG), 2015 and 2016

Source: Economic Commission for Latin America and the Caribbean (ECLAC), on the basis of figures from JP Morgan.

Economic activity

Economic growth in the region contracted yet further in 2016, while there continued to be large differences between the countries

Economic performance has differed between South America and Central America

The contraction of regional GDP reflects the persistent decline of investment and consumption

This contraction of economic activity took place in a context where the agriculture, mining and service sectors reinforced the negative contribution of industry to growth

Economic growth in the region contracted yet further in 2016, while there continued to be large differences between the countries

The GDP of Latin America and the Caribbean contracted by 1.1% in 2016, which translates into a 2.2% decline in per capita GDP. This negative rate of GDP growth continues the process of economic slowdown and contraction that the region has been mired in since 2011.

The loss of dynamism in the region's economic activity in 2016 was essentially due to lower growth in most of the South American economies and outright contractions in some, such as Argentina (-2.0%), the Bolivarian Republic of Venezuela (-9.7%), Brazil (-3.6%) and Ecuador (-2.0%). In South America as a subregion, a contraction of 1.7% in 2015 was followed by one of 2.4% in 2016.

Growth likewise slowed in the group comprising Central America,[1] where it declined from 4.7% in 2015 to 3.6% in 2016, and in Mexico, where it dropped by half a percentage point to 2.0% in 2016 from the 2.5% recorded in 2015 (see figure III.1). The economies of the English- and Dutch-speaking Caribbean contracted for the second year running (-1.7%).

Figure III.1
Latin America and the Caribbean: GDP growth rates, 2016[a]
(Percentages based on dollars at constant 2010 prices)

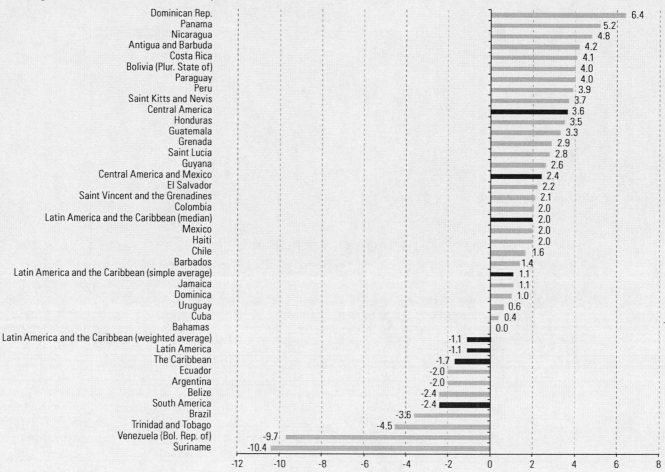

Source: Economic Commission for Latin America and the Caribbean (ECLAC), on the basis of official figures.
[a] The figures are projections.

---

[1] Includes Costa Rica, Cuba, Dominican Republic , El Salvador, Guatemala, Haiti, Honduras, Nicaragua and Panama.

The Dominican Republic and Panama are the economies of the region that grew most strongly (by 6.4% and 5.2%, respectively), followed by Nicaragua (4.8%), Antigua and Barbuda (4.2%) and then Costa Rica (4.1%). Other than Suriname, Trinidad and Tobago and Belize, which contracted by 10.4%, 4.5% and 2.4%, respectively, all the other economies grew by between 0% and 4.0% (see figure III.1).

Economic performance has differed between South America and Central America

Figure III.2
Latin America: year-on-year changes in quarterly GDP, weighted averages, first quarter of 2008 to second quarter of 2016
(Percentages based on dollars at constant 2010 prices)

Quarterly figures reveal the divergent performance of the different subregions and the contrasting trends obtaining in South America and in the group of countries formed by Central America. Growth rates in South America have declined constantly since the first quarter of 2010, first because of the loss of dynamism in the external sector and then because of the contraction of domestic demand. Conversely, recovery in the United States meant that an upturn began in the second half of 2013 both in Central America and in Mexico (see figure III.2).

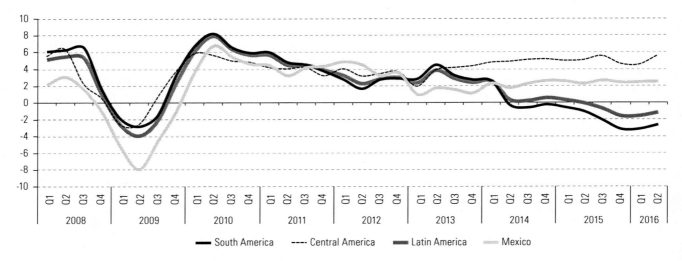

Source: Economic Commission for Latin America and the Caribbean (ECLAC), on the basis of official figures.

The contraction of regional GDP reflects the persistent decline of investment and consumption

The region's negative growth was caused mainly by a large drop in investment and consumption. Regionwide, domestic demand is estimated to have fallen by 2% in 2016, with all its components contracting: private consumption (-0.9%), public consumption (-1.0%) and gross fixed capital formation (-6.8%). In this last case, the main explanatory factors were the contraction of activity in the construction sector in some countries and the general decline in machinery and equipment investment. The contraction of private consumption reflects, first, the higher jobless rate and the worsening composition of employment and, second, a loss of dynamism in financial system lending (see chapter V, which deals with employment and wages). The drop in public consumption resulted from a general intensification of the retrenchment in public spending. A slowdown in exports, which are estimated to have grown by less than 1% in real terms in 2016, meant that their contribution, while still positive, was much smaller. Meanwhile, imports dropped by about 3% because of weaker domestic demand, which contributed positively to output growth (see figure III.3).

Figure III.3
Latin America: GDP growth rates and contribution by expenditure components to growth,
first quarter of 2008 to second quarter of 2016
(Percentages)

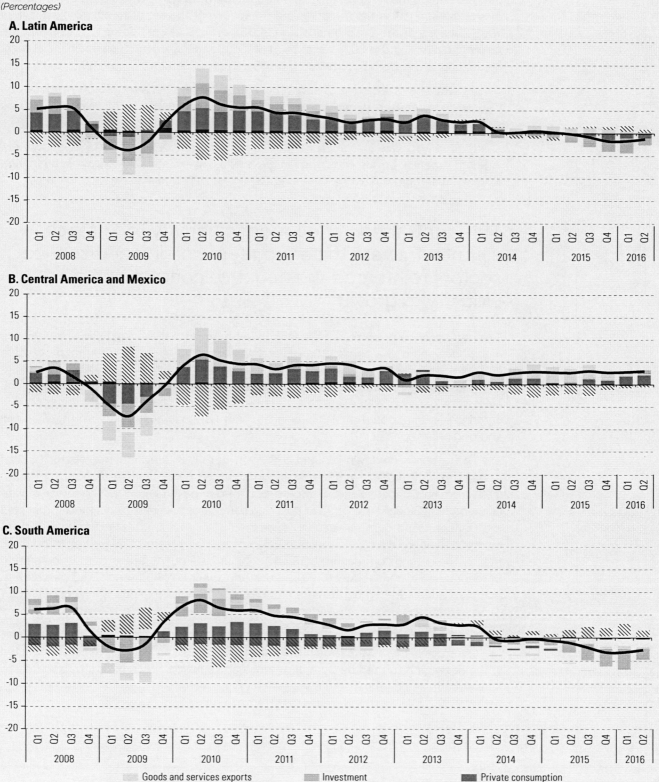

A. Latin America

B. Central America and Mexico

C. South America

Goods and services exports   Investment   Private consumption
General government consumption   Goods and services imports   GDP

Source: Economic Commission for Latin America and the Caribbean (ECLAC), on the basis of official figures.

Gross fixed capital formation has presented negative growth rates since the second quarter of 2014, so that the end of 2016 marked the eleventh consecutive quarter of decline. Prior to this, investment had only contributed negatively to GDP growth in years of economic crisis in the region: in 1995 because of the Mexican economic crisis, in 1999 because of the Brazilian crisis, in 2002 because of the "dotcom" crisis and the Argentine crisis, and in 2009 because of the international economic and financial crisis originating in the United States subprime mortgage market.

As with the divergence of economic activity trends between South America and Central America, the dynamics of domestic demand components also differed by subregion in 2016.

Thus, while private consumption and investment dropped by 2.3% and 9.9%, respectively, in South America, private consumption grew by 3.0% in Central America, becoming the main source of growth, while investment also rose, albeit to a lesser extent (1.9%).

This contraction of economic activity took place in a context where the agriculture, mining and service sectors reinforced the negative contribution of industry to growth

The performance of domestic demand in Latin America was matched by the decline in economic activity at the sectoral level. For simplicity's sake, the different production activities have been grouped into three major sectors. The first includes agriculture and mining. The second, the industrial sector, covers construction, manufacturing and electricity, gas and water. The third, the service sector, encompasses transport and communications, commerce, financial and business services and communal, social and personal services.

The export slowdown brought a drop in output in the industrial sector (-3.0%) in the first half of 2016, and this was compounded by a fall in service-sector output (-1.2%), mainly because of the decline in commerce (-1.8%), reflecting lower private consumption. Sluggish exports and declining commerce and imports negatively impacted the transport and communications sector (-8.3%). Although other services did not contract, their growth did slow as public-sector spending retrenched further. In industry, the manufacturing contraction that had begun in 2014 deepened as domestic demand deteriorated. In consequence, agriculture and mining contributed -0.56 percentage points to value added growth in the first half of 2016 (with mining alone accounting for -0.50 percentage points), the industrial sector -0.08 percentage points and the service sector -0.51 percentage points (see figure III.4).

Once again, there were large subregional differences. In 2016, only mining contracted in the subregion formed by Central America and Mexico, while in South America the construction sector, the electricity, gas and water sector and the communal, social and personal services sector were the only ones to grow.

Figure III.4

Latin America: value added growth rates and contribution of economic sectors to growth, first quarter of 2008 to second quarter of 2016
(Percentages)

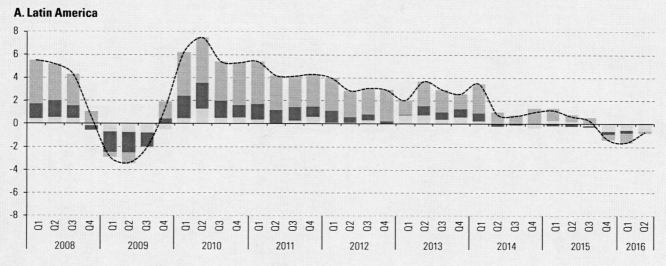

A. Latin America

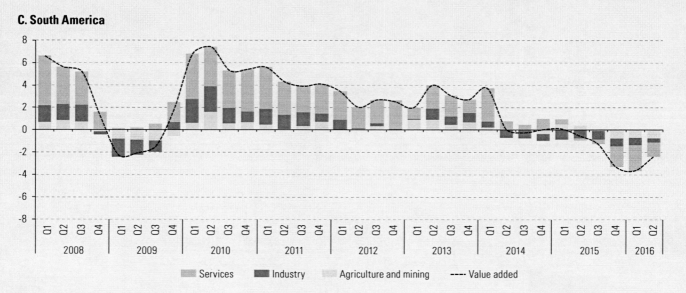

B. Central America and Mexico

C. South America

Services   Industry   Agriculture and mining   ---- Value added

Source: Economic Commission for Latin America and the Caribbean (ECLAC), on the basis of official figures.

Domestic prices

In the first nine months of 2016, inflation gathered pace in the Latin American and Caribbean economies on average, with some countries posting rates above 40%

Inflation is higher in goods than in services, while food prices are running ahead of the headline rate

In the first nine months of 2016, inflation gathered pace in the Latin American and Caribbean economies on average, with some countries posting rates above 40%

Cumulative 12-month inflation rose on average among the Latin American and Caribbean economies in the first nine months of 2016, rising from 6.9% in September 2015 to 8.4% in September 2016 (see figure IV.1).[1] This regional dynamic has been under way since inflation hit a 10-year low of 3.5% in October 2009.

Figure IV.1
Latin America and the Caribbean: consumer price index (CPI), weighted average 12-month rates of variation,
January 2011 to September 2016
(Percentages)

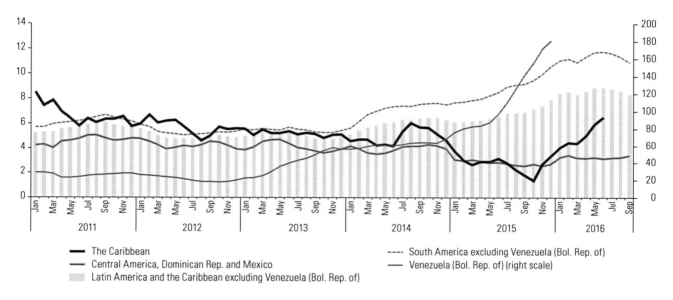

Legend:
— The Caribbean
— Central America, Dominican Rep. and Mexico
▨ Latin America and the Caribbean excluding Venezuela (Bol. Rep. of)
---- South America excluding Venezuela (Bol. Rep. of)
— Venezuela (Bol. Rep. of) (right scale)

Source: Economic Commission for Latin America and the Caribbean (ECLAC), on the basis of official figures.

Inflation has accelerated in all subregions of Latin America and the Caribbean. In South America, the 12-month cumulative rate rose from 9.2% in the September 2015 to 10.9% a year later —even though Argentina and Colombia were the only countries included in this subregional average to report higher individual rates.

The economies of Central America,[2] the Dominican Republic and Mexico, as a group, saw 12-month cumulative inflation rise from 2.5% in September 2015 to 3.4% in September 2016. Among these countries, Haiti reported the highest inflation (12.5%) and is the only one with a rate above 5%. In the English- and Dutch-speaking Caribbean economies, the 12-month cumulative rate of inflation was up by 4.5 percentage points year-on-year in September 2016 (from 1.8% to 6.3%). However, Suriname was the only economy in this subregion to post inflation of over 3% in 2016, with a rate of 63.9% in June, the highest rate for 10 years. This alone explains the rise in the subregional average rate.

---

[1] The regional and subregional averages shown in the tables and figures of this section exclude the Bolivarian Republic of Venezuela, since official information is not available on the trend of in this country in 2016.

[2] Includes Costa Rica, Cuba, El Salvador, Guatemala, Haiti, Honduras, Nicaragua and Panama.

Table IV.1
Latin America and the Caribbean: consumer price index (CPI), weighted average 12-month rates of variation,
September 2014 to September 2016
(Percentages)

	At September 2014	At September 2015	At September 2016	At December 2014	At December 2015
Latin America and the Caribbean[a]	**6.4**	**6.9**	**8.4**	**6.3**	**7.9**
South America[a]	**7.6**	**9.2**	**10.9**	**7.5**	**10.6**
Argentina	23.8	21.9	42.4[b]	23.9	27.5
Bolivia (Plurinational State of)	4.3	4.1	3.5	5.2	3.0
Brazil	6.7	9.5	8.5	6.4	10.7
Chile	5.1	4.6	3.1	4.6	4.4
Colombia	2.9	5.4	7.3	3.7	6.8
Ecuador	4.2	3.8	1.3	3.7	3.4
Paraguay	4.1	3.7	3.5	4.2	3.1
Peru	2.7	3.9	3.1	3.2	4.4
Uruguay	8.4	9.1	8.9	8.3	9.4
Venezuela (Bolivarian Republic of)	64.0	141.5	...	68.5	180.9
Central America, Dominican Republic and Mexico	**4.2**	**2.5**	**3.4**	**4.0**	**2.7**
Costa Rica	5.2	-0.9	0.4	5.1	-0.8
Cuba	1.7	2.1	...	2.1	2.8
Dominican Republic	2.8	0.4	1.4	1.6	2.3
El Salvador	1.7	-2.3	1.0	0.5	1.0
Guatemala	3.5	1.9	4.6	2.9	3.1
Haiti	5.3	11.3	12.5	6.4	12.5
Honduras	6.1	2.8	2.9	5.8	2.4
Mexico	4.2	2.5	3.0	4.1	2.1
Nicaragua	6.5	2.6	3.5	6.4	2.9
Panama	2.3	-0.4	1.2	1.0	0.3
The Caribbean	**5.7**	**1.8**	**6.3**	**4.7**	**3.3**
Antigua and Barbuda	1.6	0.9	0.0[b]	1.3	0.9
Bahamas	1.3	2.2	-0.3[b]	0.2	2.0
Barbados	2.0	-1.1	-0.4[c]	2.3	-2.5
Belize	0.9	-0.7	0.7	-0.2	-0.6
Dominica	0.9	-1.4	-0.4[b]	0.5	-0.5
Grenada	0.1	0.6	1.9[b]	-0.6	1.1
Guyana	0.3	-1.0	0.9	1.2	-1.8
Jamaica	9.0	1.8	2.2	6.2	3.7
Saint Kitts and Nevis	0.0	-2.9	-3.1[b]	-0.5	-2.4
Saint Lucia	5.5	-2.2	-4.1[b]	3.7	-2.6
Saint Vincent and the Grenadines	0.3	-1.7	0.9[b]	0.1	-2.1
Suriname	3.9	4.4	63.9[b]	3.9	25.2
Trinidad and Tobago	7.8	4.8	3.0	8.5	1.5

Source: Economic Commission for Latin America and the Caribbean (ECLAC), on the basis of official figures.
[a] Excludes the Bolivarian Republic of Venezuela owing to the lack of official information for 2016.
[b] Data as of June 2016.
[c] Data as of April 2016.

The countries with the region's highest inflation rates (Argentina, Suriname and the Bolivarian Republic of Venezuela)[3] have also been enduring steep economic downturns. Other common features of these economies include steep nominal exchange-rate depreciations, sharp public-utility rate hikes and the monetization of large fiscal deficits.

Among the economies with lower inflation (12-month cumulative rate), four English- and Dutch-speaking Caribbean countries (Bahamas, Barbados, Saint Kitts and Nevis and Saint Lucia) reported negative rates in September 2016. In Brazil and Uruguay, inflation eased in the first nine months of 2016, although it was still above 8% in both economies.

Inflation is higher in goods than in services, while food prices are running ahead of the headline rate

Although the rise in average inflation for the region has been reflected in all of its components, goods prices are outpacing services. According to figures for August 2016, the 12-month regional average rates are 10.3% and 7.8%, respectively.

Figure IV.2
Latin America and the Caribbean: consumer price index (CPI), weighted average 12-month rates of variation in headline, core, goods and services inflation, January 2011 to August 2016

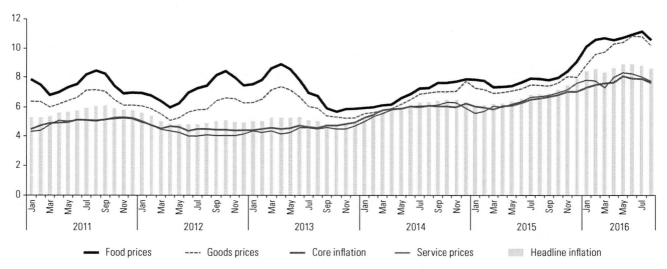

Source: Economic Commission for Latin America and the Caribbean (ECLAC), on the basis of official figures.

For the economies of South America, excluding the Bolivarian Republic of Venezuela, inflation in goods prices was up by 4.3 percentage points year-on-year in the cumulative 12-month rate in August 2016, to 13.8%, compared with 10.7% for services prices. In Central America, the Dominican Republic and Mexico, the inflation rate recorded in August 2016 was 3.3%, with service prices up 2.0%. The English- and Dutch-speaking Caribbean is the only subregion to display a different inflation dynamic; and, in this case, services outpaced goods, with prices rising by 8.7% and 6.9%, respectively.

---

[3]   Although there are no official data for the Venezuelan economy, preliminary estimates suggest a price surge in 2016, pushing inflation above the 180% recorded in the previous year. In fact, Latin America Consensus Forecast sees inflation in the Bolivarian Republic of Venezuela reaching a level of 515.4% in 2016. The factors underlying this projection include: faster growth in the monetary aggregates, driven by increasing monetization of the public sector deficit by the Central Bank of Venezuela; a steep exchange-rate depreciation, on both the official and the parallel markets; and the severe external constraint faced by this economy, which has exacerbated the dwindling supply of goods and inputs.

At the country level, goods prices rose by more than 50% in Argentina and Suriname, driven by the depreciations in their individual nominal exchange rates, whereas Saint Kitts and Nevis saw goods prices fall by 10.3%. In the case of services, Argentina and Suriname are again the leaders with prices rising by more than 40%, fuelled by higher public-utility rates and charges.

The food sector is posting the highest inflation rates, both in Latin America and the Caribbean as a whole and in each subregion. As a regional average, food price inflation was 10.7% in August 2016, 2.39 percentage points up on August 2015. In South America, food inflation was 14.4% (4.5 percentage points higher than in 2015); in Central America, the Dominican Republic and Mexico, as a group, it was 3.4%; and in the English- and Dutch-speaking Caribbean, it was 7.4%.

Employment and wages

Unemployment rose in the context of a declining employment rate and a rising participation rate

Labour market performance varied both between subregions and between men and women

Average employment quality deteriorated

Real wage growth slowed

In Latin America and the Caribbean as a whole, the quantity and quality of jobs in the labour market declined sharply during 2016. The region's urban unemployment rate increased by more than it had during the international financial crisis of 2009, and the composition of employment worsened, with the share of insecure and unprotected jobs increasing. This deterioration did not take place everywhere, though, but was concentrated in the South American countries.

Unemployment rose in the context of a declining employment rate and a rising participation rate

As regional GDP contracted, the average urban employment rate fell for the third year in a row. Having dropped by a cumulative 0.6 percentage points in 2014 and 2015, it fell even more quickly in 2016, the expectation being for a year-on-year decline to 57.1% from 57.8% in 2015.[1]

Another development in 2016 was a reversal of the downward trend in the urban participation rate that had been a feature of earlier years. In line with the predominantly procyclical behaviour of the labour supply in the region, the gradual long-run upward trend in this rate had been cut short in 2013 in response to weakening labour demand, and between 2014 and 2015 it had dropped by a cumulative 0.4 percentage points.[2] This loosening of working-age people's ties to the labour market cushioned the impact of lower job creation on the open unemployment rate. Probably because of the negative consequences of the prolonged drop in the employment rate and its impact on household incomes, however, many households began sending new members into the labour market, and this contributed to an estimated 0.3 percentage point rise in the urban participation rate in 2016.

Consequently, whereas the effects on open unemployment of developments in the participation and employment rates had partially offset each other in earlier years, they instead reinforced each other in 2016, and unemployment rose sharply (see figure V.1A).

For the year and the region as a whole, the expectation is for the urban unemployment rate to have risen from 7.4% to 9.0%. This shift represents a rise of 4.1 million in the number of urban unemployed, bringing the total number of urban residents in this situation to 21.3 million.

As can be seen in figure V.1B, covering a limited group of countries with quarterly information available, year-on-year increases in the urban unemployment rate accelerated over 2016, reaching 1.9 percentage points in the third quarter. Of particular concern is the fact that the employment rate had shown no sign of reversing its decline by that same quarter, having fallen by about 0.7 percentage points year on year in both the second and the third quarters.

---

[1] Updated information on a number of countries has been incorporated from 2016, so that the figures given in this report are not comparable with those in earlier editions. See box I.2 of the *Economic Survey of Latin America and the Caribbean 2016* for further details.
[2] Quarterly data show a year-on-year rise in the participation rate from the fourth quarter of 2015.

Figure V.1
Latin America and the Caribbean (weighted average of 12 countries): urban participation, employment and unemployment rates, rolling years and year-on-year changes, first quarter of 2013 to third quarter of 2016[a]

A. Urban participation, employment and unemployment rates, rolling years
(percentages)

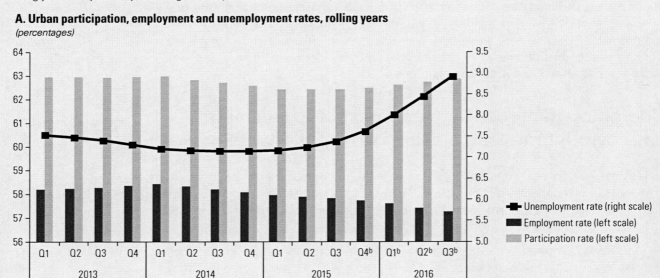

B. Year-on-year changes
(percentage points)

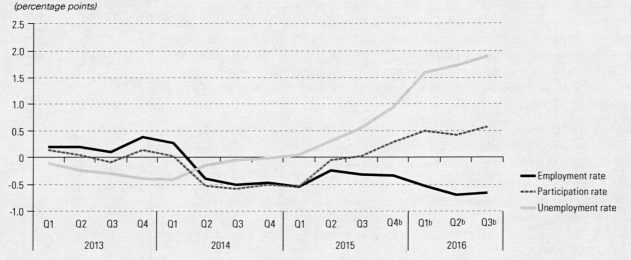

Source: Economic Commission for Latin America and the Caribbean (ECLAC), on the basis of official figures.
[a] The countries considered are Argentina, the Bolivarian Republic of Venezuela, Brazil, Chile, Colombia, Costa Rica, Ecuador, Jamaica, Mexico, Paraguay, Peru and Uruguay. Some estimates based on incomplete data are included.
[b] Preliminary data.

Labour market performance varied both between subregions and between men and women

However, labour market performance varied greatly across the different subregions. Urban unemployment rates rose to a greater or lesser degree in all the South American countries with information available (Argentina, the Bolivarian Republic of Venezuela, Brazil, Chile, Colombia, Ecuador, Paraguay, Peru and Uruguay). Thus, the urban open unemployment rate for the South American countries as a group rose from 8.2% in 2015 to 10.5% in 2016.

By contrast, open urban unemployment dropped from 4.9% to 4.6% in the group comprising Central America,[3] the Dominican Republic and Mexico and from 10.0% to 9.3% in the English-speaking Caribbean countries. According to preliminary data, this more favourable evolution was due to the rate falling in Barbados, Belize, the Dominican Republic, Jamaica and Mexico, while it held steady in Costa Rica and rose in the Bahamas, Guatemala, Panama and Trinidad and Tobago.

Thus, urban unemployment rates rose in 13 of the 19 Latin American and Caribbean countries with information available. There was a particularly large increase in Brazil, where urban unemployment in the 20 main metropolitan regions, averaged across the first three quarters, rose from 9.2% in 2015 to 12.8% in 2016. If Brazil is excluded from the regional estimate, the urban unemployment rate only rose from 6.2% to 6.5%.

Taking the simple average for these countries, the rise in the unemployment rate, averaged over the first three quarters of 2016, was 0.5 percentage points. As figure V.2 shows, this increase was more marked for women than for men (0.7 versus 0.3 percentage points), so that the gender gap for this variable widened.

Figure V.2
Latin America and the Caribbean (simple averages of 17 countries): year-on-year changes in participation, employment and unemployment rates, by sex, first three quarters of 2016[a]
(Percentage points)

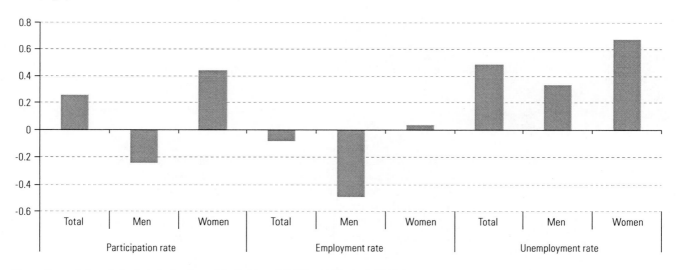

Source: Economic Commission for Latin America and the Caribbean (ECLAC), on the basis of official figures.
[a] The countries considered are Argentina, the Bahamas, Barbados, the Bolivarian Republic of Venezuela, Brazil, Chile, Colombia, Costa Rica, the Dominican Republic, Ecuador, Guatemala, Jamaica, Mexico, Panama, Paraguay, Peru and Uruguay. Not all the countries have complete information for all three quarters.

The processes driving up unemployment rates were different for men and women. In the case of men, the decisive factor was the drop in the employment rate, which outstripped the decline in the participation rate. In contrast, what predominated for women was the rise in the participation rate, while the employment rate held steady, implying a small increase in the absolute number of women in work, once again as a simple average of the countries with information available. Thus, the structural gap between the sexes narrowed for both variables.

---

[3]   In this case, the Central American countries for which information is available are Costa Rica, Guatemala and Panama.

Average employment quality deteriorated

The increase in the proportion of women in work occurred, however, in a context of worsening job quality. On the basis of information from 11 countries showing the contraction of regional output and the concomitant weakness of employers' demand for labour, it is estimated that the number of wage workers must have fallen slightly (0.2%). In contrast, own-account work continued to behave in a markedly procyclical way, rising by 2.7% (see figure V.3).[4]

Figure V.3
Latin America and the Caribbean (weighted averages for 11 countries): economic growth and job creation, 2013-2016[a]
(Percentages)

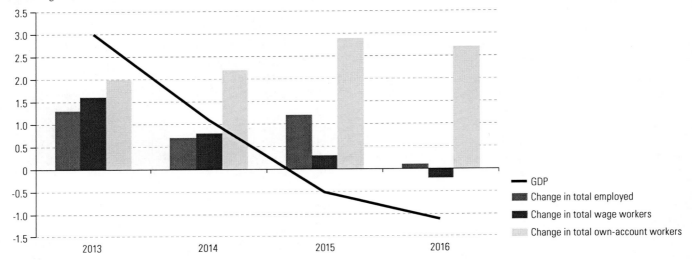

Source: Economic Commission for Latin America and the Caribbean (ECLAC), on the basis of official figures.
[a] The countries considered are the Bolivarian Republic of Venezuela, Brazil, Chile, Colombia, Costa Rica, the Dominican Republic, Ecuador, Mexico, Panama, Paraguay and Peru. The 2016 employment data are averages for the first three quarters; the 2016 GDP figure is an estimate for the year.

The weakness of labour demand and the divergent labour market performance of the different subregions were also manifested in the evolution of registered employment (employees paying into social security institutions), an indicator of good-quality employment. With the exception of Chile, where growth rates held steady, there was a sharp decrease in registered employment growth in the South American countries with information available (see figure V.4).[5] In Brazil and Uruguay, registered employment fell year on year in absolute terms.

In contrast, registered employment growth has held steady or even increased in most of the countries in the north of the region (Costa Rica, El Salvador, Mexico and Nicaragua), with Panama being an exception, as employment there contracted at larger firms in the areas of manufacturing, commerce, hotels and restaurants and other services.

The behaviour of another indicator of employment quality, hourly underemployment, was mixed.[6] This indicator of employment quality problems rose in Argentina, Chile, Ecuador, Guatemala, Peru and Uruguay, while the proportion of employed people affected by hourly underemployment fell in Colombia, Costa Rica, Mexico and Paraguay.

Job creation by branch of activity displays differences and similarities whether weighted averages or medians are used in the analysis (see figure V.5).

---

[4]   The countries with information available reported median increases of 1.1% for total employment, 0.1% for wage employment and 2.9% for own-account work.
[5]   The number of people in registered employment changes not only as such jobs are created and destroyed but as existing informal jobs become formal and formal ones become informal.
[6]   Employed people are considered to be affected by hourly underemployment when they work less than a minimum number of hours set in each country, wish to work more hours and are available to do so.

Figure V.4
Latin America (10 countries): year-on-year growth in registered employment, 2013-2016[a][b]
(Percentages)

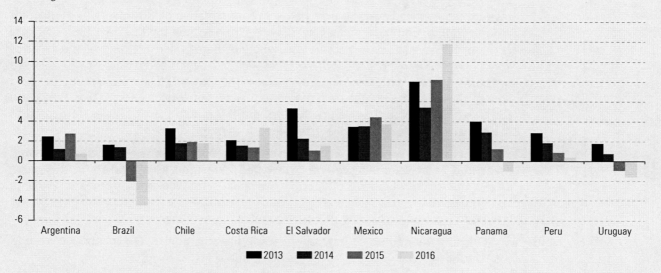

Source: Economic Commission for Latin America and the Caribbean (ECLAC), on the basis of official figures.

[a] The data are for wage workers paying into social security systems, with the exceptions of Brazil, where they are for private-sector wage workers reported by firms to the General Register of the Employed and Unemployed (CAGED); Panama, where they come from surveys of firms employing five people or more; and Peru, where they are for employment reported at small, medium-sized and large formal non-agricultural enterprises.

[b] The year-on-year changes given for 2016 are averages from January to June for Panama, January to July for El Salvador, January to August for Argentina and Nicaragua and January to September for Brazil, Chile, Costa Rica, Mexico, Peru and Uruguay.

Figure V.5
Latin America and the Caribbean (11 countries): employment changes between the first three quarters of 2015 and 2016, by branch of activity, weighted averages and medians of national rates of change[a]
(Percentages)

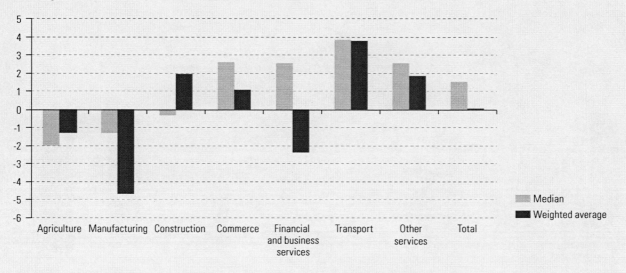

Source: Economic Commission for Latin America and the Caribbean (ECLAC), on the basis of official figures.

[a] The countries considered are Brazil, Chile, Colombia, Costa Rica, the Dominican Republic, Ecuador, Jamaica, Mexico, Panama, Paraguay and Peru.

Data from 11 countries show, first, that total employment measured as a weighted average was stagnant because of the impact of the jobs downturn in Brazil, whereas the median increased modestly. When employment by major branch of activity is taken, the weighted average also yields a more negative picture than the median for manufacturing, commerce, financial services, real estate and business services, and communal, social and personal services, whereas there is little difference in the cases of agriculture and transport. Most of the difference by major branch of activity is explained by the performance of Brazil, where employment contracted sharply in manufacturing and in the financial services, real estate and business services sector (by 10.9% and 8.6%, respectively, if the average for the first three quarters of 2016 is compared to the same period in 2015), while it held steady in commerce and construction.

Construction was the only branch where growth was more favourable when measured as a weighted average than when measured as a median. In this case, employment contracted in 5 of 11 countries because of weakening domestic demand, but employment growth in this sector in Mexico drove a moderate increase in the weighted average across the group of countries as a whole.

On both measures, in any event, employment contracted in agriculture and manufacturing while expanding, particularly, in the tertiary sector.

Real wage growth slowed

Real wages in registered employment rose by some 1% on average in the countries with information available, or about a percentage point less than in 2015 (see figure V.6A), chiefly because of higher inflation that was not offset by larger nominal increases in a context of weak demand for labour.

Figure V.6
Latin America (simple average of 10 countries): breakdown of year-on-year changes in real wages, in total and for northern and southern countries, 2015 and first three quarters of 2016[a]
(Percentages)

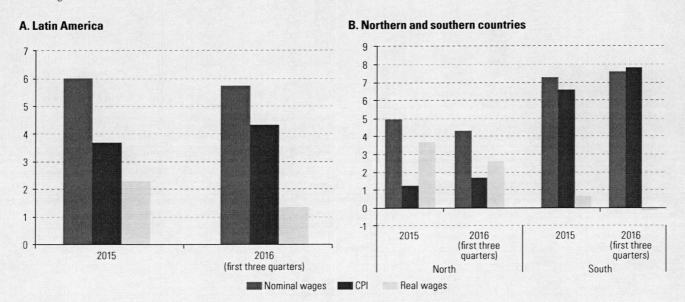

A. Latin America

B. Northern and southern countries

Legend: Nominal wages · CPI · Real wages

Source: Economic Commission for Latin America and the Caribbean (ECLAC), on the basis of official figures.
[a] The countries considered are Costa Rica, El Salvador, Mexico, Nicaragua and Panama (northern countries) and Brazil, Chile, Colombia, Peru and Uruguay (southern countries).

Differences between countries in the north and south of Latin America are in evidence once again, however. In the South American countries, following a very small increase in real wages in 2015, the rise in average year-on-year inflation in 2016 prevented them from growing again. In this group of countries, the decline in real wages in Brazil and Colombia offset small increases in Chile, Peru and Uruguay.

In contrast, the northern countries recorded a fresh increase in real wages. This was somewhat smaller than in 2015, however, because nominal increases were lower and average inflation picked up slightly.

Wage policy was dominated by the effort to stabilize wages for the least skilled workers, predominantly from low-income households, and the median minimum wage across 18 countries rose by 2.5% in real terms.

In summary, the region's macroeconomic performance affected labour markets, and job creation deteriorated sharply in the region as a whole, in terms of both quantity and quality. At the same time, the drop in the employment rate, the rise in the unemployment rate and the deteriorating composition of employment depressed households' purchasing power, which weakened the ability of domestic demand to reactivate economic growth. The small rise in the average real wage was the only factor working to stabilize households' consumption capacity. In the context of a deteriorating labour market, however, real wage increases were also smaller than in previous years.

At the same time, there was a marked difference in labour market performance between the South American countries, almost all of which suffered a deterioration of different magnitude, and countries in the other subregions, where trends were moderately more favourable.

In view of the economic growth projections for Latin America and the Caribbean in 2017, the regional employment rate is expected to remain at around the average for 2016. This implies a further increase in the regional unemployment rate if the recent trend towards a slowly rising participation rate continues, albeit only a small one of around 0.2 percentage points.

Macroeconomic policy

A. Fiscal policy

Fiscal accounts continued to follow different trends in the region's north and south during 2016

Public debt is still rising, but its growth has moderated healthily

There were deeper cutbacks in public spending, and capital spending in particular

The decline in public revenues that has been ongoing in Latin America since 2013 was aggravated in 2016 by a drop in tax receipts

B. Monetary and exchange-rate policies

Structural differences between economies and the effects of the factors mentioned above led to divergent uses being made of the different monetary policy instruments available to policymakers in the region

Lending interest rates held steady, trending slightly downward, while growth in credit to the private sector slowed

The region's currencies tended to weaken against the dollar in a context of very volatile international financial markets

The region's real effective exchange rate depreciated during 2016

International reserves rose by an average of 2.1%

A. Fiscal policy

Fiscal accounts continued to follow different trends in the region's north and south during 2016

The average fiscal deficit held steady in the countries of Latin America during 2016 relative to 2015 (see figure VI.1). This reflects a reduction in public spending that offset a fall in public revenues of 0.2 percentage points of GDP, so that the overall result came in at -3.0% of GDP for the second year running. The primary deficit (before interest payments) narrowed by 0.1 of a percentage point to -0.8% of GDP. However, differences in individual countries' macroeconomic performance and in the economic specializations of different country groupings in Latin America were reflected in a great diversity of fiscal situations.

Figure VI.1
Latin America and the Caribbean: central government fiscal indicators, 2010-2016[a]
(Percentages of GDP)

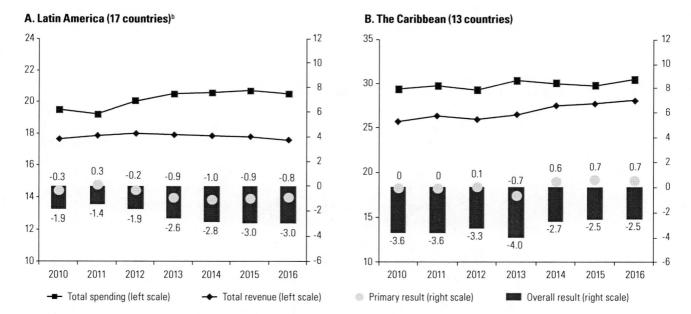

A. Latin America (17 countries)[b]

B. The Caribbean (13 countries)

— Total spending (left scale)   ◆ Total revenue (left scale)   ● Primary result (right scale)   ■ Overall result (right scale)

Source: Economic Commission for Latin America and the Caribbean (ECLAC), on the basis of official figures.
[a] The 2016 figures are official estimates for the close of the fiscal year taken from 2017 budgets.
[b] Data from the Bolivarian Republic of Venezuela, Cuba and the Plurinational State of Bolivia are excluded.

Fiscal accounts have improved in the north of the region (Central America,[1] the Dominican Republic, Haiti and Mexico), reflecting favourable terms of trade and steady growth in the United States, these countries' main trading partner. The average deficit continued to narrow in 2016, declining to -2.1% of GDP from -2.4% of GDP in 2015 (see figure VI.2). This was mainly due to a rise in public revenues (up 0.2 percentage points of GDP to 16.2% of GDP), as public spending held steady at 18.3% of GDP. It is important to note that while Mexico is a hydrocarbon exporter, the country's federal public-sector deficit also narrowed (from -3.5% to -2.9% of GDP) because of buoyant public revenues.

---

[1]   Includes Costa Rica, El Salvador, Guatemala, Honduras, Nicaragua and Panama.

Figure VI.2
Latin America (selected country groupings): central government fiscal indicators, 2010-2016[a]
(Percentages of GDP)

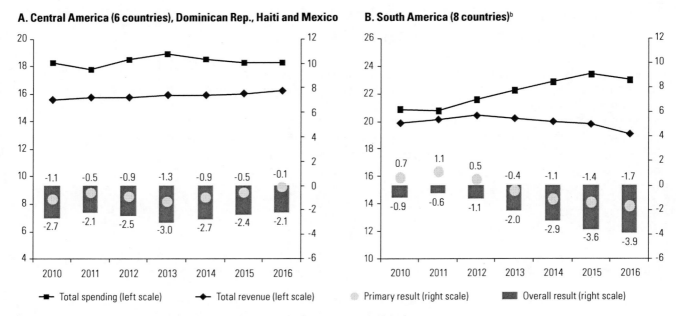

A. Central America (6 countries), Dominican Rep., Haiti and Mexico

B. South America (8 countries)[b]

- ■ Total spending (left scale)
- ◆ Total revenue (left scale)
- ● Primary result (right scale)
- ■ Overall result (right scale)

Source: Economic Commission for Latin America and the Caribbean (ECLAC), on the basis of official figures.
[a] The 2016 figures are official estimates for the close of the fiscal year taken from 2017 budgets.
[b] The countries considered are Argentina, Brazil, Chile, Colombia, Ecuador, Paraguay, Peru and Uruguay.

Conversely, the fiscal situation of the South American countries continued to worsen as international commodity prices fell and domestic demand slowed. The fiscal deficit expanded in 2016 for the fifth year running, to -3.9% of GDP from -3.6% of GDP in 2015. The first reduction in public spending as a share of GDP in five years (from 23.4% to 23.0% of GDP) was not enough to compensate for the slump in public revenues (particularly those from non-renewable natural resources), whose downward trend worsened in 2016 with a decline to 19.1% of GDP from 19.8% in 2015.

The average fiscal deficit in the English- and Dutch-speaking Caribbean held steady at -2.5% of GDP for the second year running. Higher public spending (up from 29.9% to 30.5% of GDP) was accompanied by a similar increase in public revenues (up from 27.5% to 28.1% of GDP). The average primary result remained in surplus (0.7% of GDP), reflecting both the large share of total spending accounted for by interest payments and the commitment of governments in the subregion to reducing their high levels of public borrowing.

Public debt is still rising, but its growth has moderated healthily

Gross public debt across all countries of Latin America continued on its upward trend to average 37.9% of GDP in 2016, a rise of 1.3 percentage points of GDP on 2015. This trend was seen in 14 of the region's 19 countries, with Brazil having the highest public debt at 70.3% of GDP, followed by Argentina at 54.0% of GDP, Honduras at 45.9% and Uruguay at 44.8%. At the other extreme, Chile's public debt is the region's lowest at 20.6% of GDP, followed by Paraguay at 20.9% and Peru at 21.7%.

It is important to include holdings of financial assets in the region, since for some countries they are substantial, so that net debt figures provide a clearer picture of each country's net financial position. The countries holding the largest portfolios of financial assets in 2016 were Brazil, Chile and Uruguay, where they were worth about 24% of GDP. Thus, Brazil had net general government debt of 45.8% of GDP, equivalent to some 65% of its gross debt. Chile, meanwhile, had net central government debt of -3.3% of GDP, as it had more assets than gross liabilities in 2016, while Uruguay had net debt of 20.4% of GDP, or roughly half its gross debt. These countries were followed by Argentina, Colombia, Ecuador, Mexico and Peru with lower values (see figure VI.3).

Figure VI.3
Latin America and the Caribbean: gross and net central government debt, 2015-2016[a]
(Percentages of GDP)

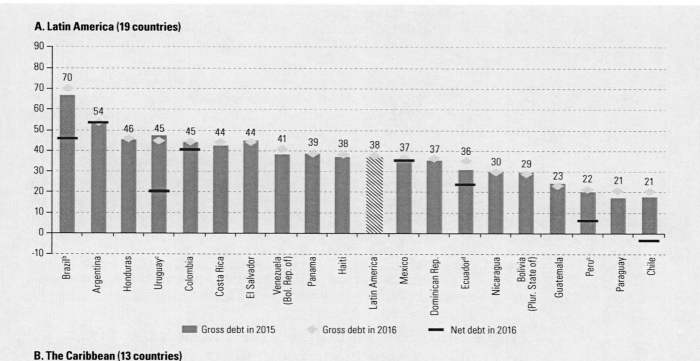

A. Latin America (19 countries)

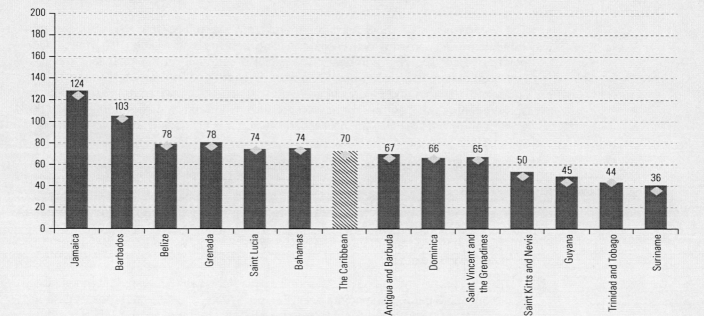

B. The Caribbean (13 countries)

Source: Economic Commission for Latin America and the Caribbean (ECLAC), on the basis of official figures.
[a] Net debt is defined as gross debt minus financial assets. For 2016, the latest figure available is given.
[b] General government coverage.
[c] Non-financial public-sector coverage for net debt.
[d] Net debt equals consolidated debt.

Although the level of public debt in the region increased on average in 2016, its growth slowed to 1.3 percentage points of GDP from the 2.9 percentage points of GDP recorded in 2015. This was because the countries opted on the whole to borrow relatively moderately and keep the public accounts sustainable by trimming public spending to offset the decline in public revenues.

At the subregional level, gross public debt increased by 1.9 percentage points of GDP in South America, with Ecuador (4.9 percentage points of GDP), Brazil (3.8 points) and Paraguay (3.6 points) seeing the largest increases. The debt level in Central America was very similar to that in 2015, averaging about 37% of GDP, with increases in Costa Rica (2.0 percentage points of GDP) and Haiti (1.7 points), as well as the Dominican Republic (1.5 points).

Central government debt in the English- and Dutch-speaking Caribbean averaged 69.6% of GDP in 2016, a drop of 2 percentage points of GDP from 2015. Jamaica was the country with the highest level of public debt in 2016 (124% of GDP), followed by Barbados (103% of GDP) and Belize (78% of GDP). Although debt levels are still quite high in many countries of the region, the overall trend is downward, since there were declines in 10 of the 13 countries, most particularly Antigua and Barbuda, Guyana, Jamaica and Suriname.

The cost of debt held steady relative to 2015, averaging 2% of GDP in Latin America. The country with the highest interest payments was Brazil, where they were about 5% of GDP, although this was 2.2 percentage points of GDP less than in 2015, followed by Colombia, Costa Rica, the Dominican Republic and Honduras, where the cost was 3% of GDP. At the other extreme, Chile and Paraguay paid less than 1% of GDP in interest. The cost of public debt in the Caribbean was 3.2% of GDP because of high debt levels. Barbados and Jamaica were the countries where debt service represented the greatest cost to the fiscal accounts, at over 8% of GDP.

There were deeper cutbacks in public spending, and capital spending in particular

The figures available show certain general trends in public spending. Budget cuts continued in Latin America, with capital spending dropping by an average of 0.3 percentage points of GDP across a number of the region's countries, the largest falls being in hydrocarbon-exporting countries (Colombia, Ecuador and Trinidad and Tobago) and in Argentina, Panama and Paraguay (see figure VI.4). Public investment rose sharply in some countries of Central America (Guatemala, Honduras and Nicaragua) and in the Caribbean. There was also an increase in Mexico, mainly because of capital transfers to Petróleos Mexicanos (PEMEX).

There have been no substantial increases in public debt service, with most countries' interest payments remaining broadly unchanged. Only Argentina, Colombia and Honduras present increases of more than 0.5 percentage points of GDP. Interest payments in Brazil underwent a large correction in 2016, dropping by 2.2 percentage points of GDP, mainly because of the monetary adjustment resulting from falling inflation (3.8 percentage points down on the 2015 rate), which corrected short-term debt costs downward.

Current primary spending held steady in most of the Latin American countries, rising by a modest 0.2 percentage points of GDP or so in food-exporting countries (Argentina, Paraguay and Uruguay) and the Caribbean. In Brazil, the increase was 0.5 percentage points of GDP. In the Central American countries and Mexico, conversely, current primary spending dropped by 0.1 and 0.8 percentage points of GDP, respectively. In hydrocarbon-exporting countries (Colombia, Ecuador and Trinidad and Tobago), this decline was 0.7 percentage points of GDP.

Figure VI.4
Latin America and the Caribbean: disaggregated central government spending, by subregion
and country grouping, 2015-2016[a]
(Percentages of GDP)

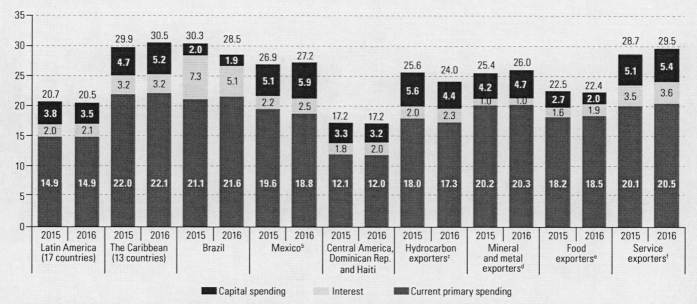

Source: Economic Commission for Latin America and the Caribbean (ECLAC), on the basis of official figures.
a The 2016 figures are official estimates for the close of the fiscal year taken from 2017 budgets.
b Federal public sector.
c Colombia, Ecuador and Trinidad and Tobago.
d Chile, Guyana, Peru and Suriname.
e Argentina, Paraguay and Uruguay.
f Antigua and Barbuda, Bahamas, Barbados, Belize, Dominica, Grenada, Jamaica, Panama, Saint Kitts and Nevis, Saint Lucia
and Saint Vincent and the Grenadines.

The decline in public revenues that has been ongoing in Latin America since 2013 was aggravated in 2016 by a drop in tax receipts

Public revenues as a share of GDP in Latin America continued a decline that had begun in 2013 (see figure VI.1). The trend intensified in 2016, however, with a drop of 0.2 percentage points of GDP to 17.6% of GDP on average for the 17 countries with information available (see figure VI.5). This was partly due to a fall in tax receipts (0.2 percentage points of GDP), something not seen since 2009. Nonetheless, the averages given here tend to mask a high degree of heterogeneity in the region's results.

Public revenues, particularly tax receipts, dropped substantially in South America owing to both the negative effects of the cycle and falling prices for the commodities exported by the countries. In Brazil, public revenues fell by 0.4 percentage points of GDP overall, but the drop in tax receipts was greater (0.8 percentage points of GDP). In Argentina, likewise, a drop of 1.0 percentage point of GDP in the tax take was largely responsible for a decline of 1.2 percentage points of GDP in total revenues.

In Central America, the Dominican Republic, Haiti and Mexico, public revenues held steady or even grew. They were particularly strong in El Salvador (up 0.4 percentage points of GDP), where they were driven by income tax receipts, and Haiti (0.6 percentage points of GDP), where local tax receipts in Port-au-Prince rose strongly. Public revenues rose in Mexico (0.9 percentage points of GDP) despite a fresh decline in oil revenues, thanks to a rise in the income tax take and a one-off increase in the income of the Federal Electricity Commission (CFE) because of a change in its pension regime.

Figure VI.5
Latin America and the Caribbean: disaggregated central government revenues, by subregion and country grouping, 2015-2016[a]
(Percentages of GDP)

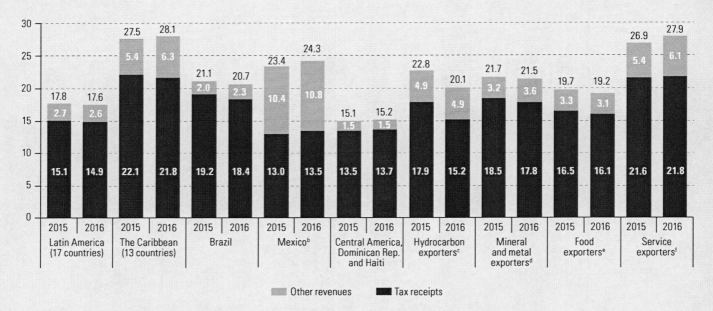

Source: Economic Commission for Latin America and the Caribbean (ECLAC), on the basis of official figures.
[a] The 2016 figures are official estimates for the close of the fiscal year taken from 2017 budgets.
[b] Federal public sector.
[c] Colombia, Ecuador and Trinidad and Tobago.
[d] Chile, Guyana, Peru and Suriname.
[e] Argentina, Paraguay and Uruguay.
[f] Antigua and Barbuda, Bahamas, Barbados, Belize, Dominica, Grenada, Jamaica, Panama, Saint Kitts and Nevis, Saint Lucia and Saint Vincent and the Grenadines.

Notwithstanding a drop in tax receipts of 0.3 percentage points of GDP, public revenues in the English- and Dutch-speaking Caribbean rose by 0.6 percentage points of GDP to 28.1% of GDP because of growth in other income, mainly subsidies for investment projects.

Further price declines for hydrocarbons and for minerals and metals negatively affected public-sector receipts in countries exporting these. Public revenues dropped by an average of 2.7 percentage points of GDP in hydrocarbon-exporting countries, mainly because of a drop of the same size in tax receipts. Oil revenues in Trinidad and Tobago, consisting mainly of income tax payments, fell greatly in 2016 as the sector lost profitability in the country, although the base of comparison was high because the State firm Petrotrin paid off tax arrears in 2015. Central government oil revenues in Colombia, consisting mainly of income tax payments and dividend payments by Ecopetrol, were close to zero because of the loss posted by Ecopetrol in 2015.

Public revenues in mineral- and metal-exporting countries also fell, by 0.2 percentage points of GDP. Public revenues in Chile dropped by 0.3 percentage points of GDP, mainly because of lower tax receipts. It is important to emphasize that this outcome in Chile reflects both the large fall in the tax take from the private mining sector and a high basis of comparison in 2015, when revenues were boosted by a tax amnesty. The fall in total revenues in Peru (0.9 percentage points of GDP) is explained by a reduction in tax receipts (a lower VAT take and a rise in rebates) and non-tax revenues (particularly mining and hydrocarbon royalties). Tax receipts also dropped substantially in Guyana and Suriname (by 0.9 and 0.8 percentage points of GDP, respectively), again dragging total revenues down.

The tax take as a share of GDP dropped in almost half the region's countries with information available (13 of 27) in 2016. As figure VI.6 illustrates, the tax burden dropped in Latin America at the central government level (for the first time since 2009) from 15.1% to 14.9% of GDP. This was due to the trend in South America, since tax receipts continued to move upward in the north of the region (Central America, the Dominican Republic, Haiti and Mexico). Tax receipts fell on average in the Caribbean after rising for two years, from 22.1% to 21.8% of GDP. Although this decline centred on just a few countries, tax receipts in the other countries of the subregion were not as dynamic as in the previous period.

Figure VI.6
Latin America and the Caribbean: central government tax burdens, 2007-2016[a]
(Percentages of GDP)

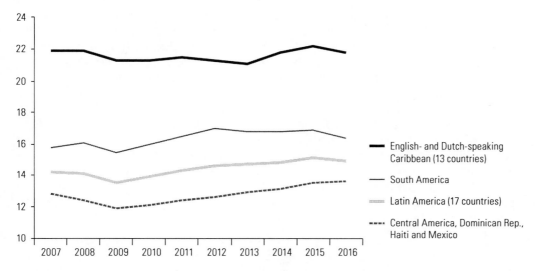

- **English- and Dutch-speaking Caribbean (13 countries)**
- South America
- Latin America (17 countries)
- Central America, Dominican Rep., Haiti and Mexico

Source: Economic Commission for Latin America and the Caribbean (ECLAC), on the basis of official figures.
[a] The 2016 figures are official estimates for the close of the fiscal year taken from 2017 budgets.

B. Monetary and exchange-rate policies

During 2016, as already discussed in the 2016 *Economic Survey*, the actions of those directing monetary and exchange-rate policies in the region were guided by different factors, chief among them the dynamics of inflation, uncertainty and thence volatility in international financial markets and weak growth (and even contraction in some cases) in aggregate demand.

Broadly speaking, the authorities of the region's countries paid a great deal of attention to the aggregate demand slowdown and the repercussions of variables such as consumption and investment. Accordingly, the aim of policy was to stimulate domestic aggregate demand as far as possible.

The region's average inflation rate increased during 2016, reducing the scope for monetary policymakers to take steps to stimulate aggregate demand. Similarly, the volatility of financial markets and the repercussions for exchange rates in the region likewise limited the potential for interest rates to be used to stimulate domestic spending, as it was feared that this would dampen demand for local assets. Meanwhile, less buoyant economic activity and expectations of low future growth, especially in the economies of South America, also affected central banks' ability to stimulate aggregate domestic demand, partly by dampening growth in the demand for credit and partly by increasing the perceived riskiness of lending and thus constraining the supply of credit.

Structural differences between economies and the effects of the factors mentioned above led to divergent uses being made of the different monetary policy instruments available to policymakers in the region

In economies that use interest rates as the main instrument of monetary policy, there were differences in the frequency and direction of changes to monetary policy benchmark rates during the first 10 months of 2016. In some countries, persistently rising inflation led central banks to increase interest rates, while in others inflation fell and interest rates were used to stimulate flagging activity in the domestic economy.

Interest rates moved most often in Colombia, Mexico and Paraguay, but in different directions and for different reasons (see figure VI.7). In Colombia, rising inflation meant that in 2016 the benchmark interest rate increased eight times by a total of 225 basis points from its level at the close of 2015. In Mexico, the benchmark rate was raised four times, with a cumulative rise of 200 basis points, the trigger in this case being uncertainty about monetary policy in the United States and, more recently, that country's presidential elections. In Paraguay, the benchmark rate was cut twice following an increase in February 2016, giving a cumulative decline of 25 basis points from the end-2015 level and 50 basis points from its value in February 2016. In Peru, the benchmark rate was increased in the first quarter of 2016 and then left unchanged, while in Brazil it was cut by 25 basis points in October 2016, the first change since July 2015. In both economies, these movements were a response to inflation rising above its target band and to political and electoral events. In Chile, Costa Rica, the Dominican Republic and Guatemala, lesser inflationary pressures meant that benchmark rates were left unchanged in the first 10 months of 2016.

Something else worth highlighting is that benchmark monetary policy rates in economies such as Brazil, Colombia, Mexico and Peru are at their highest for five years, whereas in Chile, Costa Rica, the Dominican Republic, Guatemala and Paraguay they are currently close to their lowest levels since 2011.

In Latin American economies that use monetary aggregates as their main monetary policy instrument, the rate at which central banks injected money into the economy slowed in the first three quarters of 2016. This meant that the nominal growth of the monetary base slackened in the South American economies (excluding the Bolivarian Republic of Venezuela), in the group formed of Central America (including only non-dollarized economies) and the Dominican Republic and in the region's dollarized economies (see figure VI.8). In the economies of the English- and Dutch-speaking Caribbean, the growth of aggregates such as the monetary base quickened slightly relative to 2015.

In the case of the Bolivarian Republic of Venezuela, the monetary aggregates grew at rates of over 80% for the third year running. Indeed, annualized growth in the monetary base was over 100% in the first three quarters of 2016, reaching 130% in the third quarter.

Figure VI.7
Latin America (selected countries): monetary policy rates in countries where they are used
as the main policy instrument, January 2013 to October 2016
(Percentages)

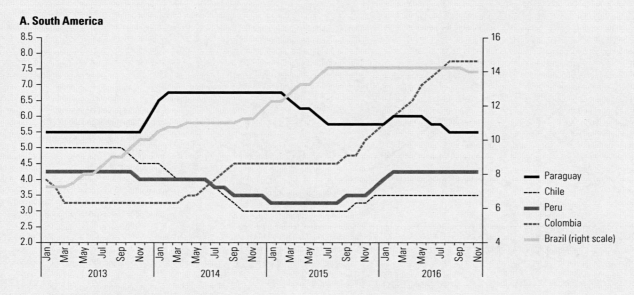

A. South America

B. Central America, Dominican Rep. and Mexico

Source: Economic Commission for Latin America and the Caribbean (ECLAC), on the basis of official figures.

Figure VI.8
Latin America and the Caribbean (selected country groupings): annualized rates of change
in the monetary base in countries using monetary aggregates as the main policy instrument,
first quarter of 2010 to third quarter of 2016
(Percentages)

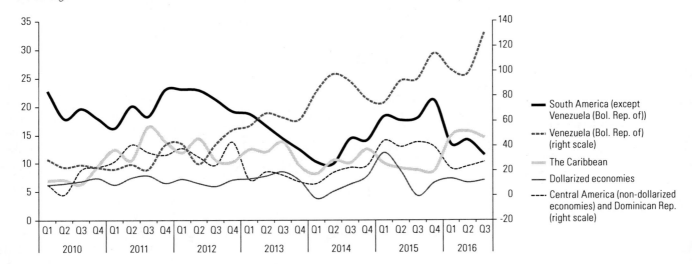

Source: Economic Commission for Latin America and the Caribbean (ECLAC), on the basis of official figures.

Lending interest rates held steady, trending slightly downward, while growth in credit to the private sector slowed

The policies described above yielded fairly stable market interest rates, although there was a slight downward trend in most of the region's economies. The exceptions were the economies of South America that employ the monetary policy rate as their main policy instrument, as market rates there increased slightly during 2016 (see figure VI.9).

Figure VI.9
Latin America and the Caribbean (selected country groupings): average annualized lending interest rates, January 2010 to September 2016
(Percentages)

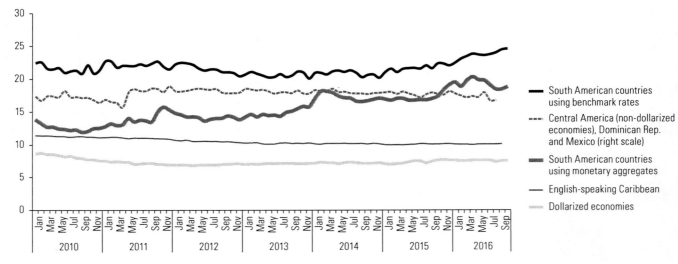

Source: Economic Commission for Latin America and the Caribbean (ECLAC), on the basis of official figures.

One salient fact is that both lending interest rates and monetary policy benchmark rates in Brazil and Colombia have recently reached levels that are among the highest recorded since 2011, while in most of the other economies lending interest rates have recently been below the average for the period between January 2011 and September 2016.[2]

Where domestic lending to the private sector is concerned, nominal growth has tended to slacken. In South America, real-term lending growth has slowed both in economies that use benchmark rates as the main monetary policy instrument and in those using monetary aggregates. By contrast, real-term lending has edged up in real terms in the group comprising Central America (including only non-dollarized economies), the Dominican Republic and Mexico, as it has in the dollarized economies. Real-term credit to the private sector dropped sharply in the Bolivarian Republic of Venezuela during the first three quarters of 2016, reflecting the harsh contraction experienced by this economy and three-digit inflation rates (see figure VI.10).

Figure VI.10
Latin America and the Caribbean (selected country groupings): average annualized rates of growth in domestic lending to the private sector, real terms, first quarter of 2013 to third quarter of 2016
(Percentages)

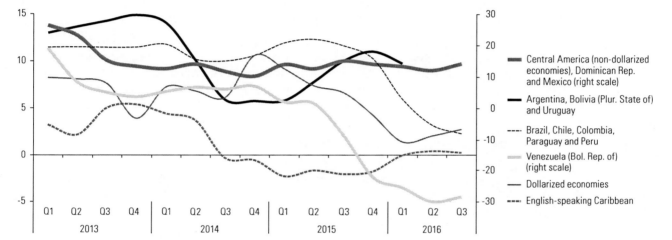

Source: Economic Commission for Latin America and the Caribbean (ECLAC), on the basis of official figures.

Other striking developments in the first nine months of 2016 were the considerable drop in commercial lending in the South American economies that use aggregates as the main monetary policy instrument and in lending to industrial sectors in the South American economies that use benchmark rates as the main instrument.

The lending dynamic could be reflecting the influence of slowing aggregate demand growth in the region. For one thing, lower economic growth has caused the supply of credit to increase more slowly, since adverse growth expectations can make lending riskier. For another, lower income growth combined with expectations of a slow recovery, less dynamic consumption and slow growth in private investment have been bearing down on the demand for credit from the private sector, even though lending interest rates have been trending slightly downward.

The region's currencies tended to weaken against the dollar in a context of very volatile international financial markets

A number of factors affected the exchange rates of the region's currencies in 2016, and the trend was broadly towards nominal depreciation, albeit with great volatility over the year. Since 2015, factors such as falling prices for the commodities the region

---

[2]   The exceptions are Argentina, the Bolivarian Republic of Venezuela, the Dominican Republic, Ecuador, El Salvador, Trinidad and Tobago and Uruguay.

exports (particularly energy products and metals), the strengthening of the dollar against currencies elsewhere in the world at a time of rising expectations of an increase in the United States benchmark interest rate (which did finally go up in December 2015) and slowing growth in a number of South American countries, together with specific events in countries such as Argentina and Brazil, have driven down demand for assets denominated in the currencies of a number of the region's countries.

The international context remained uncertain in the first 10 months of 2016, and factors such as the outcome of the referendum in the United Kingdom on the country's exit from the European Union (so-called "Brexit"), uncertainty about new monetary policy adjustments in the developed economies, reports of increasing fragility in global financial institutions and, more recently, the presidential elections in the United States all affected the dynamics of Latin American and Caribbean exchange rates. Furthermore, expectations for the price levels of commodities such as oil, copper and other metals progressively stabilized in this period. The exchange rates of the region's currencies also reflected the effects of rising monetary policy benchmark rates in response to higher inflation (in Brazil and Colombia), at a time of slowing growth.

The conjunction of these external and domestic factors meant that, comparing values for November 2016 with those for December 2015, the currencies of 13 countries in the region depreciated against the dollar in nominal terms, 5 of them by more than 15% (Argentina, the Bolivarian Republic of Venezuela, Haiti, Mexico and Suriname) (see table VI.1).

Table VI.1
Latin America and the Caribbean (21 countries): annualized changes in nominal dollar exchange rates, 2014 to November 2016
(Percentages)

Country	2014	2015	December 2015 to March 2016	March 2016 to June 2016	June 2016 to September 2016	September 2016 to 18 November 2016	December 2015 to 18 November 2016
Latin America							
Argentina	29.8	52.8	13.7	2.3	1.7	1.1	19.7
Bolivia (Plurinational State of)	0.0	-0.1	-1.2	1.3	0.0	0.4	0.5
Brazil	12.5	49.0	-9.3	-10.6	1.5	3.9	-14.4
Chile	15.4	16.8	-5.8	-0.7	-0.9	3.2	-4.2
Colombia	23.2	33.6	-5.4	-2.7	-1.3	10.2	0.0
Costa Rica	7.6	-0.4	0.2	1.9	0.9	0.2	3.2
Dominican Republic	4.0	2.5	0.7	0.2	0.3	0.7	1.9
Guatemala	-3.1	0.5	1.0	-0.9	-1.5	-0.3	-1.8
Haiti	8.1	20.0	10.1	1.5	4.0	1.4	17.8
Honduras	3.8	6.4	1.2	0.7	1.1	0.5	3.5
Mexico	13.2	16.6	0.4	5.8	6.0	5.4	18.7
Nicaragua	5.0	5.0	1.0	1.6	0.4	0.8	3.8
Paraguay	0.8	24.7	-2.7	-0.7	-0.6	4.4	0.3
Peru	6.5	14.6	-3.0	-0.7	2.9	0.6	-0.3
Uruguay	13.1	23.0	6.0	-3.5	-7.0	2.4	-2.6
Venezuela (Bolivarian Republic of)[a]	0.0	58.7	36.5	130.2	4.9	0.2	229.9
The Caribbean							
Belize	1.0	-0.8	0.0	0.0	0.0	0.0	0.0
Guyana	-0.1	0.2	0.0	0.0	0.0	0.0	0.0
Jamaica	7.9	4.9	1.3	4.1	0.8	1.4	7.8
Suriname	3.8	16.8	27.7	38.5	8.9	-5.6	81.9
Trinidad and Tobago	-0.6	0.8	2.8	0.7	1.0	0.5	5.0

Source: Economic Commission for Latin America and the Caribbean (ECLAC), on the basis of information from Bloomberg.
[a] The Bolivarian Republic of Venezuela has multiple exchange rates. The figure is for changes in the "complementary currency" (DICOM) exchange rate for non-priority exports.

Figure VI.11 presents the evolution of nominal dollar exchange-rate indices for Argentina, Haiti and Mexico from January 2014 to November 2016.[3] In Argentina, following unification of the currency market in December 2015, the peso generally showed a slight tendency towards depreciation and some volatility, especially in the first half of 2016, as a number of policy measures were implemented to correct the fiscal dominance problem bequeathed by the outgoing government. In Haiti, the gourde continued to be affected by the country's large current account deficit and uncertainty about external financing flows of different kinds (including Petrocaribe), as well as by specific problems such as hurricane Matthew. In the case of Mexico, a particular factor was the exchange-rate volatility associated with the United States election period during 2016. In Suriname, a major terms-of-trade shock and monetary financing of the fiscal deficit led to a drop in demand for domestic assets, high inflation and, in consequence, a large currency depreciation. In the Bolivarian Republic of Venezuela, lastly, the different bolívar exchange rates depreciated in the context of one of the world's highest inflation rates, a general scarcity of goods, rapid growth in monetary aggregates and a large decline in GDP.

Figure VI.11
Argentina, Haiti and Mexico: nominal dollar exchange-rate indices, January 2014 to November 2016
(Base January 2008=100)

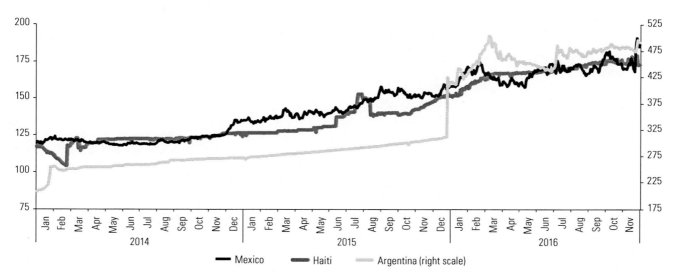

Source: Economic Commission for Latin America and the Caribbean (ECLAC), on the basis of official figures.

Another important factor is what could be characterized as the volatility of currencies over the year, with analysis of currency developments in the region bringing to light different patterns as 2016 progressed. Table VI.1 and figure VI.12 show movements in the exchange rates of some of the region's currencies over 2016. The table shows quarterly dynamics, while the chart presents a more detailed picture of the five economies that best exemplify this volatility. In both it can be seen that the currencies of several economies in the region appreciated in the first three quarters of 2016, only for this movement to be wholly or partly reversed in September and November. Indeed, the chart shows that the trend moved towards depreciation following the results of the United States elections.

---

[3]   Data for the Bolivarian Republic of Venezuela are not included because the country has multiple exchange rates applying in different segments of the economy, which gives rise to problems of comparison.

Figure VI.12
Brazil, Chile, Colombia, Paraguay and Uruguay: nominal dollar exchange-rate indices, January 2014 to November 2016
(Base January 2008=100)

Source: Economic Commission for Latin America and the Caribbean (ECLAC), on the basis of official figures.

The region's real effective exchange rate depreciated during 2016

The real effective extraregional exchange rate of 18 countries of Latin America and the Caribbean depreciated by an average of 1.9% in the first 10 months of 2016 relative to the same period in 2015. The economies of South America experienced an effective depreciation against the rest of the world of 1.5%, while there was a 2.2% aggregate depreciation in the other subregions (Central America, the Dominican Republic, Mexico and the Caribbean), heavily influenced by an effective depreciation of 14.7% in Mexico. When October 2016 is compared to October 2015, however, South America is found to have experienced an effective appreciation of 6.8%, owing to nominal appreciation in countries such as Brazil, Colombia and Uruguay, among others, as already described (see figure VI.13).

Figure VI.13
Latin America and the Caribbean (18 countries): effective extraregional exchange-rate indices by subregion,
January 2014 to October 2016
(Base 2005=100)

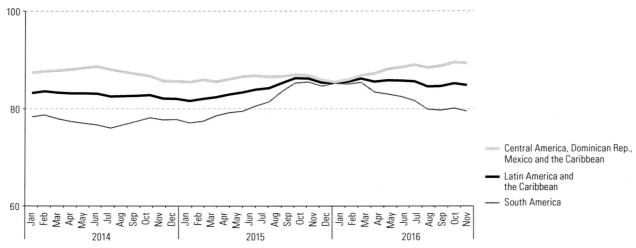

Source: Economic Commission for Latin America and the Caribbean (ECLAC), on the basis of official figures.

The evolution of the total effective exchange rate[4] of the region's countries reflects in particular the above-mentioned changes in the nominal exchange rates of each country and of all trading partners plus the evolution of inflation in each country, as described in the relevant section of this report. Particular mention should be made of countries with less flexible exchange rates, where there was real effective appreciation during the period. This was the case with the Plurinational State of Bolivia (where there was a 5.7% appreciation in the first 10 months of the year), whose exchange rate has been acting as an inflation anchor, Ecuador (2.2%), Panama (1.1%) and El Salvador (0.3%). The exception was Trinidad and Tobago, where there was a total effective depreciation of 0.6%. Mention should also be made of Guatemala: it had higher inflation than the United States, its nominal exchange rate appreciated slightly and the currencies of its largest trading partners depreciated, the result being a real effective appreciation of 5.5% for the country during the period.

International reserves rose by an average of 2.1%

International reserves increased slightly (by 2.1%) in the first 11 months of 2016 relative to the end of 2015. However, they remained below their 2014 level (see figure VI.14). Reserves increased in 22 of the region's economies, with the largest rises occurring in Ecuador (61.6%), Argentina (46.9%), Saint Kitts and Nevis (22.3%), Dominica (25.0%) and El Salvador (25.0%). Meanwhile, reserves contracted in 10 countries, most notably the Bolivarian Republic of Venezuela (28.2%), the Plurinational State of Bolivia (20.3%), Belize (-14.7%) and Uruguay (11.7%). Among the economies with the highest levels of international reserves, particular mention should be made of increases in Brazil and Chile, amounting to 2.6% and 2.1%, respectively.

Figure VI.14
Latin America and the Caribbean: international reserves, 2000-2016[a]
(Billions of dollars and percentages of GDP)

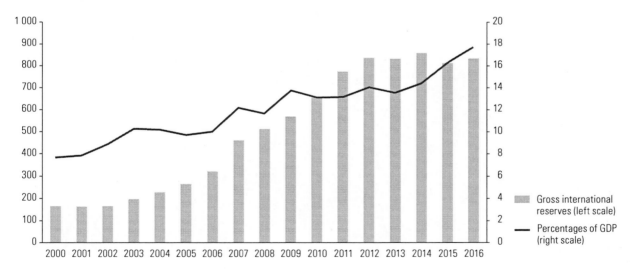

Gross international reserves (left scale)

Percentages of GDP (right scale)

Source: Economic Commission for Latin America and the Caribbean (ECLAC), on the basis of official figures.
a The 2015 figures are ECLAC estimates. The 2016 figures are for October and contain preliminary data.

The conjunction of a larger build-up of nominal reserves and low economic growth has pushed up the ratio of international reserves to GDP in the region as a whole, so that this indicator rose for the fourth year running, to 17.7% of GDP.

---

4   Unlike the effective extraregional exchange rate, which excludes trade with the Latin American and Caribbean countries from the weighting, the total effective exchange rate takes account of trade with all the trading partners of each country.

Risks and outlook for 2017

Global risks and uncertainties in 2107 will have diverse effects on the region's economic performance. Sluggish growth of the global economy, which has now been a reality for over a decade, with average growth of 2.5% in the period 2013-2016, will continue: the average projected for 2017-2018 is 2.8%. This slack performance has been accompanied by slowing productivity —which shows a growth rate of around 1%— and declining rates of growth in global investment and trade. These factors, together with depressed aggregate demand, are holding down the growth potential of the world economy —across developed countries and emerging economies alike— for the next few years.

Although trade is projected to pick up somewhat in 2017 —by between 1.8% and 3.1%, better than the 1.7% in 2016— the effects of this improvement may be overshadowed by the mounting protectionism seen since the United Kingdom voted to leave the European Union (Brexit). One positive feature is that commodity prices are projected to rise by 8% on average in 2017. The strongest recovery is expected in energy products, whose prices should gain around 19%, while other products will see a price rise of some 2%.

In financial markets, the windows of opportunity opened by the low interest rates that have prevailed over the past few years may begin to close, owing to expected rises in interest rates (the United States Federal Reserve will likely raise its rate by between 0.5% and 0.75%), which would push up borrowing costs and shift global portfolios. A normalization of interest rates, though desirable, could increase uncertainly and financial volatility, given the dynamics of financial asset prices. Although the likelihood remains that interest rate rises will be gradual, this could still affect financial flows to emerging markets, including those of Latin America and the Caribbean. Concerns also persist over the financial stability of economies in which credit, especially in the form of international bond issues, has grown strongly, since these could be hurt by higher interest rates on dollar liabilities.

This is in addition to concerns over the position of a number of financial institutions in developed countries —chiefly in the eurozone— which have not been able to restore their balance sheets to health since the global financial crisis and have, moreover, seen their profits eroded by years of low growth and low interest rates. The results of stress tests carried out in mid-2016 by the European Banking Authority (EBA) have not fully dispelled doubts about the real situation of banks in some eurozone countries.

Recent protectionist trends, amid complex financial and economic growth dynamics, have raised new uncertainties and risks regarding the future of the global economy. These trends reflect the mounting tensions and difficulties in reconciling and coordinating national policy emphases and aims with the institutional arrangements governing international movements of goods and services, finance and capital, technology and migration in a globalized world.

In this context, global trade —following the questioning of free trade agreements such as the Trans-Pacific Partnership (TPP) and the North American Free Trade Agreement (NAFTA)— is not the only area of tension. The value chain dynamics of global manufacturing, as well as technology mobility, will also be affected. Multilateralism could well be weakened by a stronger tendency towards bilateral agreements on trade and investment.

As in preceding years, global economic conditions will have different effects on the various countries and subregions of Latin America and the Caribbean, and will sharpen subregional differences by the production and trade orientation of their economies. Although the protectionist tendencies emerging in the United States will have global and regional effects, the possible renegotiation of NAFTA and other trade agreements, as well as uncertainty over the dynamics of monetary transfers from migrants, will have significant effects in particular on Mexico and Central America, which export most of their manufactures and services to the United States (81% in the case of Mexico, 41% for Costa Rica, 47% for El Salvador, 36% for Guatemala, 44% for Honduras, and 54% for Nicaragua). For the region, therefore, any trade restrictions introduced in the United States will at least partly offset the positive effects of growth in trade with that country.

For the region overall, extraregional demand should pick up in 2017, although this could be dampened to some extent by trade decisions by the United States. Intraregional trade should also regain some ground in 2017, thanks to a stronger performance by the economies of the South America, especially Argentina and Brazil. The performance of the economies in the south of the region should benefit from the projected upturn in their terms of trade, although uncertainty remains over the economic future of the eurozone and China.

The subpar performance of domestic demand across the region in 2016 was attributable mainly to a heavy drop in investment and consumption by both public and private sectors, although with sharp differences between subregions. While in South America private consumption and investment dropped by 2.3% and 9.9%, respectively, in Central America private consumption expanded by 3.0% and investment by 1.9%. Some of these trends should improve in 2017, with stronger private consumption and investment.

As noted earlier, growth in the region reflects uncertainty and shocks coming from the international economy, on the one hand, and a heavy fall in domestic consumption and investment, on the other. Regaining a growth path will require reversing these trends, with an emphasis on investment, which in turn will require strong mobilization of financial resources. The growing difficulties faced by the countries of the region in financing countercyclical fiscal policy, added to their status as middle-income countries —which hinders their access to external concessional financing and to international cooperation funding—, mean that mobilizing domestic and external resources to finance investment must be a policy priority for the countries in the near term.

To regain fiscal space, it is essential to reduce tax evasion and avoidance and to gradually reform the public finances to safeguard the solvency of the public sector, protect investment, lock in social progress and broaden tax resources. ECLAC estimates that tax evasion and avoidance cost the region the equivalent of 2.4 percentage points of GDP in the case of VAT and 4.3 percentage points in the case of income tax. This represented a total of US$ 340 billion in 2015, or 6.7% of regional GDP. ECLAC also estimates that tax losses associated with illicit financial flows from the region have amounted to around US$ 31 billion over the past few years, or between 10% and 15% of actual personal income tax collection.

Budget adjustments involving cuts in public investment could deepen the recessionary conditions, because this investment, like private investment, plays a key role in short- and long-run growth. Estimates show that fiscal multipliers are high and significant in the region, and that the public investment multiplier is higher than 2 after two years.

Unlike in 2016 when the region contracted by 1.1%, and despite complex external conditions and a number of risks, in 2017 the region's economy is expected to switch direction and return positive growth of 1.3% (see table VII.1), thanks mainly to the expected upturn in the terms of trade and in international trade volumes. As in 2016, however, the weighted average growth figure masks different growth dynamics between countries and subregions. Central America, including the Spanish-speaking Caribbean and Haiti, is expected grow by around 3.7% in 2017; including Mexico, with a projected growth rate of 1.9%, brings the average down to 2.3%. Positive growth is projected in 2017 for South America, at 0.9%, and for the English-speaking Caribbean, at 1.3%.

Table VII.1
Latin America and the Caribbean: annual growth in gross domestic product, 2011-2017
(Percentages, on the basis of dollars at constant 2010 prices)

Country	2011	2012	2013	2014	2015	2016[a]	2017[b]
Argentina	6.0	-1.0	2.4	-2.5	2.5	-2.0	2.3
Bolivia (Plurinational State of)	5.2	5.1	6.8	5.5	4.8	4.0	3.8
Brazil	3.9	1.9	3.0	0.1	-3.9	-3.6	0.4
Chile	5.8	5.5	4.0	1.9	2.3	1.6	2.0
Colombia	6.6	4.0	4.9	4.4	3.1	2.0	2.7
Costa Rica	4.5	5.2	2.0	3.0	3.7	4.1	3.9
Cuba	2.8	3.0	2.7	1.0	4.3	0.4	0.9
Dominican Republic	3.1	2.8	4.7	7.6	7.0	6.4	6.2
Ecuador	7.9	5.6	4.9	4.0	0.2	-2.0	0.3
El Salvador	2.2	1.9	1.8	1.4	2.5	2.2	2.2
Guatemala	4.2	3.0	3.7	4.2	4.1	3.3	3.3
Haiti	5.5	2.9	4.2	2.8	1.7	2.0	1.0
Honduras	3.8	4.1	2.8	3.1	3.6	3.5	3.4
Mexico	4.0	4.0	1.4	2.2	2.5	2.0	1.9
Nicaragua	6.2	5.6	4.5	4.6	4.9	4.8	4.7
Panama	11.8	9.2	6.6	6.1	5.8	5.2	5.9
Paraguay	4.3	-1.2	14.0	4.7	3.0	4.0	3.8
Peru	6.3	6.1	5.9	2.4	3.3	3.9	4.0
Uruguay	5.2	3.5	4.6	3.2	1.0	0.6	1.0
Venezuela (Bolivarian Republic of)	4.2	5.6	1.3	-3.9	-5.7	-9.7	-4.7
Subtotal de América Latina	**4.5**	**2.9**	**2.9**	**0.9**	**-0.5**	**-1.1**	**1.3**
Antigua and Barbuda	-1.8	3.8	-0.2	4.6	4.1	4.2	2.9
Bahamas	0.6	3.1	0.0	-0.5	-1.7	0.0	1.0
Barbados	0.8	0.3	-0.1	0.2	0.5	1.4	1.9
Belize	2.1	3.7	1.3	4.1	1.2	-2.4	3.7
Dominica	-0.2	-1.1	0.8	4.2	-1.8	1.0	3.2
Grenada	0.8	-1.2	2.4	7.3	6.2	2.9	2.6
Guyana	5.4	4.8	5.2	3.8	3.0	2.6	3.8
Jamaica	1.7	-0.6	0.5	0.7	1.0	1.1	1.2
Saint Kitts and Nevis	2.4	-0.6	6.2	6.0	3.8	3.7	5.3
Saint Lucia	0.2	-1.4	0.1	0.4	1.9	2.8	2.3
Saint Vincent and the Grenadines	-0.4	1.4	1.8	1.2	1.6	2.1	2.2
Suriname	5.3	3.1	2.9	1.8	-2.0	-10.4	0.8
Trinidad and Tobago	-0.3	1.3	2.3	-1.0	0.2	-4.5	0.5
Subtotal for the Caribbean	**1.0**	**1.3**	**1.5**	**0.4**	**0.4**	**-1.7**	**1.3**
Latin America and the Caribbean	**4.5**	**2.8**	**2.9**	**0.9**	**-0.5**	**-1.1**	**1.3**
Central America (9 countries)[c]	**4.4**	**4.0**	**3.7**	**3.9**	**4.7**	**3.6**	**3.7**
South America (10 countries)[d]	**4.7**	**2.5**	**3.3**	**0.3**	**-1.8**	**-2.4**	**0.9**

Source: Economic Commission for Latin America and the Caribbean (ECLAC), on the basis of official figures.
[a] Estimates.
[b] Projections.
[c] Includes Costa Rica, Cuba, Dominican Republic, El Salvador, Guatemala, Haiti, Honduras, Nicaragua and Panama.
[d] Includes Argentina, Bolivarian Republic of Venezuela, Brazil, Chile, Colombia, Ecuador, Paraguay, Peru, Plurinational State of Bolivia and Uruguay.

Statistical annex

Table A1.1

Latin America and the Caribbean: main economic indicators

	2007	2008	2009	2010	2011	2012	2013	2014	2015	2016[a]
	Annual growth rates									
Gross domestic product[b]	5.8	4.1	-1.7	6.2	4.5	2.8	2.9	0.9	-0.5	-1.1
Per capita gross domestic product[b]	4.5	2.7	-2.9	4.9	3.3	1.7	1.7	-0.2	-1.6	-2.2
Consumer prices[c]	5.6	7.0	3.5	5.4	5.8	4.9	5.0	6.3	7.9	8.4
	Percentages									
Urban open unemployment	8.6	8.0	9.2	8.6	7.8	7.4	7.2	7.0	7.4	9.0
Total gross external debt/GDP[d e]	31.9	29.0	29.9	27.6	26.5	28.4	30.2	32.6	34.9	36.4
Total gross external debt/exports of goods and services	82.5	75.8	99.4	96.4	89.2	96.9	102.6	113.2	133.5	150.4
	Millions of dollars									
Balance of payments[e]										
Current account balance	-8 599	-27 581	-34 487	-107 366	-122 850	-132 729	-158 445	-188 849	-179 185	-105 314
Exports of goods f.o.b.	766 565	881 042	714 303	898 126	1 099 819	1 116 240	1 099 371	1 083 333	924 085	864 955
Imports of goods f.o.b.	735 930	849 178	676 877	864 779	1 045 732	1 079 149	1 099 969	1 105 630	984 700	879 484
Services trade balance	-17 907	-33 258	-37 009	-51 729	-67 387	-73 821	-73 372	-75 298	-52 864	-38 185
Income balance	-101 006	-113 856	-107 864	-148 300	-172 339	-158 148	-146 933	-157 068	-133 735	-124 741
Net current transfers	66 009	67 211	59 364	59 315	62 789	62 149	62 457	65 854	68 029	71 722
Capital and financial balance[f]	144 090	63 600	85 833	187 526	210 919	185 728	168 060	219 328	150 938	125 098
Net foreign direct investment	96 000	103 021	72 157	110 405	153 484	148 447	142 086	142 354	134 795	499
Other capital movements	48 090	-39 421	13 676	77 121	57 436	37 281	25 974	76 973	16 143	124 599
Overall balance	134 933	38 879	51 712	83 160	91 758	58 688	16 477	37 907	-26 345	6 981
Variation in reserve assets[g]	-135 600	-42 872	-57 543	-80 270	-97 146	-59 217	-19 195	-40 175	23 780	-21 559
Other financing	667	3 993	5 831	-3 032	5 048	407	2 206	2 272	2 534	0
Net transfer of resources	43 751	-46 263	-16 201	36 195	43 628	27 986	23 333	64 531	19 737	392
International reserves	459 581	512 727	567 444	655 305	773 632	835 735	830 018	857 438	811 762	829 202
	Percentages of GDP									
Fiscal sector[h]										
Overall balance	0.1	-0.4	-2.7	-1.9	-1.4	-1.9	-2.6	-2.8	-3.0	-3.0
Primary balance	2.1	1.3	-0.9	-0.3	0.3	-0.2	-0.9	-1.0	-0.9	-0.8
Total revenue	17.8	18.1	17.0	17.6	17.8	18.0	17.9	17.8	17.8	17.6
Tax revenue	14.2	14.2	13.6	13.9	14.4	14.7	14.8	14.8	15.1	14.9
Total expenditure	17.6	18.5	19.7	19.5	19.2	20.0	20.5	20.6	20.7	20.5
Capital expenditure	3.1	3.7	3.8	4.0	3.8	4.2	4.3	4.0	3.8	3.5
Central-government public debt	30.3	28.8	30.9	29.8	29.0	30.5	32.3	33.6	36.5	37.9
Public debt of the non-financial public-sector	32.3	30.9	33.2	32.4	31.3	32.7	34.6	36.2	39.4	40.7

Source: Economic Commission for Latin America and the Caribbean (ECLAC), on the basis of official figures.
[a] Preliminary figures.
[b] Based on official figures expressed in 2010 dollars.
[c] December-December variation. Weighted average, does not include the Bolivarian Republic of Venezuela.
[d] Estimates based on figures denominated in dollars at current prices.
[e] Does not include the Caribbean, Cuba and the Bolivarian Republic of Venezuela.
[f] Includes errors and omissions.
[g] A minus sign (-) indicates an increase in reserve assets.
[h] Coverage corresponds to the central government. Simple averages for 19 countries.

Table A1.2
Latin America and the Caribbean: gross domestic product in millions of dollars
(Current prices)

	2007	2008	2009	2010	2011	2012	2013	2014	2015	2016[a]
Latin America and the Caribbean[b]	**5.8**	**4.1**	**-1.7**	**6.2**	**4.5**	**2.8**	**2.9**	**0.9**	**-0.5**	**-1.1**
Latin America	**5.8**	**4.1**	**-1.6**	**6.3**	**4.5**	**2.9**	**2.9**	**0.9**	**-0.5**	**-1.1**
Argentina	9.0	4.1	-5.9	10.1	6.0	-1.0	2.4	-2.5	2.5	-2.0
Bolivia (Plurinational State of)	4.6	6.1	3.4	4.1	5.2	5.1	6.8	5.5	4.8	4.0
Brazil	6.1	5.1	-0.1	7.5	3.9	1.9	3.0	0.1	-3.9	-3.6
Chile	4.6	3.7	-1.0	5.8	5.8	5.5	4.0	1.9	2.3	1.6
Colombia	6.9	3.5	1.7	4.0	6.6	4.0	4.9	4.4	3.1	2.0
Costa Rica	7.9	2.7	-1.0	5.0	4.5	5.2	2.0	3.0	3.7	4.1
Cuba	7.3	4.1	1.5	2.4	2.8	3.0	2.7	1.0	4.3	0.4
Dominican Republic	8.5	3.2	0.9	8.3	3.1	2.8	4.7	7.6	7.0	6.4
Ecuador	2.2	6.4	0.6	3.5	7.9	5.6	4.9	4.0	0.2	-2.0
El Salvador	3.8	1.3	-3.1	1.4	2.2	1.9	1.8	1.4	2.5	2.2
Guatemala	6.3	3.3	0.5	2.9	4.2	3.0	3.7	4.2	4.1	3.3
Haiti	3.3	0.8	3.1	-5.5	5.5	2.9	4.2	2.8	1.7	2.0
Honduras	6.2	4.2	-2.4	3.7	3.8	4.1	2.8	3.1	3.6	3.5
Mexico	3.1	1.4	-4.7	5.1	4.0	4.0	1.4	2.2	2.5	2.0
Nicaragua	5.3	2.9	-2.8	3.2	6.2	5.6	4.5	4.6	4.9	4.8
Panama	12.1	8.6	1.6	5.8	11.8	9.2	6.6	6.1	5.8	5.2
Paraguay	5.4	6.4	-4.0	13.1	4.3	-1.2	14.0	4.7	3.0	4.0
Peru	8.5	9.1	1.1	8.3	6.3	6.1	5.9	2.4	3.3	3.9
Uruguay	6.5	7.2	4.2	7.8	5.2	3.5	4.6	3.2	1.0	0.6
Venezuela (Bolivarian Republic of)	8.8	5.3	-3.2	-1.5	4.2	5.6	1.3	-3.9	-5.7	-9.7
The Caribbean	**6.5**	**1.4**	**-3.6**	**1.3**	**0.9**	**1.1**	**1.4**	**0.3**	**0.2**	**-1.7**
Antigua and Barbuda	9.3	0.0	-12.0	-7.0	-1.8	3.8	-0.2	4.6	4.1	4.2
Bahamas	1.4	-2.3	-4.2	1.5	0.6	3.1	0.0	-0.5	-1.7	0.0
Barbados	1.7	0.3	-1.5	0.3	0.8	0.3	-0.1	0.2	0.5	1.4
Belize	1.1	3.2	0.8	3.3	2.1	3.7	1.3	4.1	1.2	-2.4
Dominica	6.4	7.1	-1.2	0.7	-0.2	-1.1	0.8	4.2	-1.8	1.0
Grenada	6.1	0.9	-6.6	-0.5	0.8	-1.2	2.4	7.3	6.2	2.9
Guyana	7.0	2.0	3.3	4.4	5.4	4.8	5.2	3.8	3.0	2.6
Jamaica	17.1	-0.7	-4.4	-1.5	1.7	-0.6	0.5	0.7	1.0	1.1
Saint Kitts and Nevis	-0.2	6.3	-3.0	-2.2	2.4	-0.6	6.2	6.0	3.8	3.7
Saint Lucia	1.0	4.2	-0.4	-1.7	0.2	-1.4	0.1	0.4	1.9	2.8
Saint Vincent and the Grenadines	2.4	2.5	-2.1	-3.4	-0.4	1.4	1.8	1.2	1.6	2.1
Suriname	5.1	4.1	3.0	5.2	5.3	3.1	2.9	1.8	-2.0	-10.4
Trinidad and Tobago	4.5	3.4	-4.4	3.3	-0.3	1.3	2.3	-1.0	0.2	-4.5

Source: Economic Commission for Latin America and the Caribbean (ECLAC), on the basis of official figures.
[a] Preliminary figures.
[b] Based on official figures expressed in dollars at constant 2010 prices.

Table A1.3
Latin America and the Caribbean: per capita gross domestic product
(Annual growth rates)

	2007	2008	2009	2010	2011	2012	2013	2014	2015	2016[a]
Latin America and the Caribbean[b]	**4.5**	**2.7**	**-2.9**	**4.9**	**3.3**	**1.7**	**1.7**	**-0.2**	**-1.6**	**-2.2**
Latin America	**4.4**	**2.8**	**-2.9**	**4.9**	**3.3**	**1.7**	**1.7**	**-0.2**	**-1.6**	**-2.2**
Argentina	7.9	3.0	-6.9	9.0	4.9	-2.1	1.3	-3.5	1.5	-2.9
Bolivia (Plurinational State of)	2.8	4.3	1.6	2.4	3.5	3.4	5.1	3.8	3.2	2.4
Brazil	4.8	3.9	-1.2	6.4	2.9	0.9	2.1	-0.8	-4.7	-4.4
Chile	3.4	2.5	-2.1	4.6	4.7	4.3	2.9	0.8	1.2	0.6
Colombia	5.6	2.3	0.5	2.8	5.5	3.0	3.8	3.4	2.2	1.1
Costa Rica	6.5	1.3	-2.3	3.6	3.2	3.9	0.9	1.9	2.7	3.0
Cuba	7.2	4.1	1.4	2.3	2.7	2.8	2.6	0.9	4.2	0.4
Dominican Republic	7.0	1.8	-0.4	6.9	1.8	1.5	3.5	6.3	5.8	5.2
Ecuador	0.5	4.6	-1.1	1.8	6.2	4.0	3.3	2.4	-1.3	-3.4
El Salvador	3.4	0.9	-3.5	1.0	1.8	1.5	1.4	1.0	2.0	1.8
Guatemala	3.9	1.0	-1.6	0.7	2.0	0.8	1.6	2.1	2.1	1.3
Haiti	1.7	-0.7	1.5	-6.9	4.0	1.4	2.8	1.4	0.3	0.7
Honduras	4.3	2.4	-4.1	2.1	2.2	2.6	1.3	1.6	2.2	2.1
Mexico	1.5	-0.3	-6.2	3.5	2.5	2.6	0.0	0.9	1.1	0.7
Nicaragua	3.9	1.5	-4.0	1.9	4.9	4.3	3.3	3.4	3.8	3.7
Panama	10.2	6.7	-0.1	4.0	9.9	7.4	4.9	4.4	4.1	3.6
Paraguay	4.0	4.9	-5.2	11.6	2.9	-2.6	12.5	3.3	1.6	2.7
Peru	7.2	7.8	-0.1	7.0	4.9	4.7	4.4	1.0	1.9	2.6
Uruguay	6.3	6.8	3.9	7.5	4.8	3.2	4.3	2.9	0.6	0.2
Venezuela (Bolivarian Republic of)	7.0	3.6	-4.7	-2.9	2.7	4.2	-0.0	-5.1	-6.9	-10.8
The Caribbean	**5.7**	**0.6**	**-4.3**	**0.6**	**0.2**	**0.5**	**0.7**	**-0.3**	**-0.4**	**-2.3**
Antigua and Barbuda	8.1	-1.1	-13.0	-8.0	-2.8	2.8	-1.2	3.5	3.1	3.1
Bahamas	-0.5	-4.1	-5.8	-0.2	-1.0	1.5	-1.4	-1.9	-2.9	-1.2
Barbados	1.3	-0.1	-1.9	-0.1	0.4	0.0	-0.4	-0.1	0.2	1.1
Belize	-1.5	0.6	-1.7	0.9	-0.3	1.4	-0.9	1.9	-1.0	-4.4
Dominica	6.2	7.0	-1.3	0.4	-0.6	-1.5	0.3	3.7	-2.2	0.5
Grenada	5.8	0.6	-6.9	-0.9	0.4	-1.5	1.9	6.9	5.8	2.4
Guyana	6.7	1.6	3.0	4.0	5.1	4.5	4.9	3.5	2.6	2.1
Jamaica	16.6	-1.2	-4.9	-1.9	1.3	-1.0	0.2	0.3	0.6	0.7
Saint Kitts and Nevis	-1.5	5.0	-4.2	-3.4	1.2	-1.8	4.9	4.7	2.6	2.6
Saint Lucia	-0.5	2.6	-1.8	-2.9	-0.8	-2.3	-0.7	-0.4	1.2	2.0
Saint Vincent and the Grenadines	2.3	2.4	-2.2	-3.4	-0.4	1.4	1.8	1.1	1.5	2.0
Suriname	4.1	3.0	1.8	4.0	4.2	2.1	1.9	0.9	-2.9	-11.2
Trinidad and Tobago	4.0	2.9	-4.8	2.8	-0.8	0.8	1.8	-1.5	-0.2	-4.8

Source: Economic Commission for Latin America and the Caribbean (ECLAC), on the basis of official figures.
[a] Preliminary figures.
[b] Based on official figures expressed in dollars at constant 2010 prices.

Table A1.4
Latin America and the Caribbean: gross fixed capital formation[a]
(Percentages of GDP)

	2007	2008	2009	2010	2011	2012	2013	2014	2015	2016[b]
Latin America and the Caribbean	**19.3**	**20.3**	**19.3**	**20.2**	**21.1**	**21.3**	**21.3**	**20.8**	**19.4**	**18.4**
Argentina	16.9	17.6	14.5	16.6	18.4	17.3	17.3	16.5	15.6	15.5
Bahamas	27.9	25.8	24.3	24.0	25.3	27.6	26.9	30.4	27.1	...
Belize	20.1	24.9	20.1	15.3	14.9	15.7	18.2	20.1	...	...
Bolivia (Plurinational State of)	14.4	16.1	16.1	16.6	19.5	19.0	19.9	20.7	20.7	20.3
Brazil	17.9	19.1	18.7	20.5	21.1	20.8	21.4	20.4	18.3	17.4
Chile	19.4	22.4	19.9	21.0	22.8	24.1	23.7	22.3	21.5	21.5
Colombia	21.0	22.3	21.7	21.9	24.4	24.6	25.0	26.3	26.2	25.7
Costa Rica	20.5	22.1	19.9	20.0	20.8	21.4	20.7	20.7	21.7	21.0
Dominican Republic	26.8	27.6	23.3	25.1	23.7	23.0	22.4	23.3	26.3	28.3
Ecuador	22.1	24.1	23.1	24.6	26.1	27.3	28.7	28.7	27.0	25.6
El Salvador	16.9	15.8	13.2	13.3	14.8	14.3	15.4	14.2	15.0	...
Guatemala	19.7	18.0	15.6	14.8	15.2	15.3	15.0	15.0	15.2	15.3
Haiti	25.1	25.6	25.7	25.4	...	...	...	...	...	...
Honduras	32.7	33.3	22.1	21.6	24.3	24.2	23.1	22.1	...	...
Mexico	22.3	23.1	22.0	21.2	21.9	22.1	21.4	21.6	21.9	21.7
Nicaragua	23.8	23.9	19.4	21.4	24.4	27.3	28.0	26.9	31.0	31.0
Panama	27.5	29.5	28.2	30.2	33.7	37.3	42.2	43.7	...	...
Paraguay	13.7	15.2	14.7	15.9	16.9	15.8	15.5	16.1	16.0	15.9
Peru	18.7	21.9	20.9	23.5	24.3	26.3	26.2	25.1	22.7	22.0
Uruguay	17.6	19.6	17.7	19.1	19.4	22.1	22.0	21.8	19.8	19.4
Venezuela (Bolivarian Republic of)	21.3	20.7	19.6	18.7	18.7	21.9	19.6	17.0	17.5	4.1

Source: Economic Commission for Latin America and the Caribbean (ECLAC), on the basis of official figures.
[a] Based on official figures expressed in dollars at constant 2010 prices.
[b] Preliminary figures.

Table A1.5
Latin America and the Caribbean: balance of payments
(Millions of dollars)

	Exports of goods f.o.b.			Exports of services			Imports of goods f.o.b.			Imports of services		
	2014	2015	2016[a]	2014	2015	2016[a]	2014	2015	2016[a]	2014	2015	2016[a]
Latin America and the Caribbean	1 083 333	924 085	...	154 521	151 296	...	1 105 630	984 700	...	229 818	204 160	...
Latin America[b]	1 061 344	906 886	837 022	143 670	140 358	139 105	1 077 274	959 749	851 097	221 269	195 997	169 364
Argentina	68 407	56 788	57 117	13 877	14 046	12 678	62 429	57 176	53 516	16 940	17 971	18 866
Bolivia (Plurinational State of)	12 810	8 673	7 025	1 231	1 242	1 166	9 888	9 004	7 743	3 024	2 810	2 670
Brazil	224 098	190 092	183 439	39 965	33 778	33 891	230 727	172 422	139 662	88 072	70 696	61 864
Chile	74 924	62 232	58 800	11 011	9 777	9 780	68 580	58 738	55 214	14 829	13 589	12 845
Colombia	56 899	38 114	32 397	6 900	7 144	7 053	61 539	52 049	43 930	13 560	11 439	9 944
Costa Rica	9 493	9 404	9 988	6 955	7 358	8 190	14 784	14 464	14 753	2 448	2 728	2 946
Dominican Republic	9 899	9 523	9 333	7 025	7 537	8 118	17 273	16 863	16 779	2 835	3 139	3 149
Ecuador	26 596	19 049	16 763	2 346	2 391	2 071	26 660	20 699	15 731	3 517	3 197	2 800
El Salvador	4 255	4 381	4 249	2 226	2 330	2 470	9 463	9 320	8 761	1 486	1 544	1 716
Guatemala	10 992	10 824	10 499	2 830	2 823	2 696	17 056	16 381	15 562	3 033	3 162	3 002
Haiti	961	1 024	1 001	701	724	651	3 666	3 445	3 223	1 085	986	888
Honduras	8 072	8 041	7 759	1 087	1 104	1 153	11 070	11 097	10 653	1 784	1 794	1 763
Mexico	397 650	381 049	369 618	21 086	22 886	22 886	400 440	395 573	386 008	33 537	32 056	30 347
Nicaragua	3 622	3 341	3 174	1 388	1 437	1 657	6 024	6 083	6 204	1 036	948	1 053
Panama	14 972	12 784	10 994	12 655	14 535	14 680	25 795	22 492	19 793	4 868	4 499	4 364
Paraguay	13 105	10 898	11 225	892	860	860	12 079	10 317	9 698	1 114	1 104	1 057
Peru	39 533	34 236	35 299	5 950	6 226	6 413	41 042	37 385	35 741	7 680	7 958	7 799
Uruguay	10 343	9 077	8 362	3 345	2 997	2 694	11 252	9 340	8 126	3 206	2 603	2 291
Venezuela (Bolivarian Republic of)	74 714	37 357	...	2 201	1 163	...	47 508	36 901	...	17 216	13 774	...
The Caribbean	21 989	17 200	...	10 850	10 937	...	28 356	24 951	...	8 549	8 163	...
Antigua and Barbuda	69	60	61	522	543	558	517	444	453	225	226	233
Bahamas[c]	834	527	...	2 717	2 737	...	3 316	2 953	...	1 725	1 271	...
Barbados	792	801	...	1 103	1 127	...	1 652	1 537	...	462	494	...
Belize[c]	589	538	...	494	496	...	926	961	...	225	221	...
Dominica	39	32	33	179	179	185	203	192	211	75	74	78
Grenada	44	38	39	189	200	202	299	307	314	104	110	112
Guyana	1 167	1 170	...	181	143	...	1 791	1 475	...	426	423	...
Jamaica	1 449	1 261	1 286	2 952	3 057	2 872	5 208	4 414	4 275	2 245	2 157	2 241
Saint Kitts and Nevis	58	60	63	315	321	340	285	370	388	139	161	169
Saint Lucia	184	207	195	448	456	464	552	502	482	191	186	185
Saint Vincent and the Grenadines	53	51	54	132	137	144	319	295	301	93	91	93
Suriname	2 145	1 652	...	211	204	...	2 012	2 028	...	761	674	...
Trinidad and Tobago	14 566	10 804	...	1 407	1 339	...	11 276	9 474	...	1 878	2 074	...

Table A1.5 (continued)

	Goods and services balance			Income balance			Current transfers balance			Current account balance		
	2014	2015	2016[a]	2014	2015	2016[a]	2014	2015	2016[a]	2014	2015	2016[a]
Latin America and the Caribbean	**-97 635**	**-113 479**	**...**	**-157 068**	**-133 735**	**...**	**65 854**	**68 029**	**...**	**-188 849**	**-179 185**	**...**
Latin America[b]	**-93 569**	**-108 502**	**-44 335**	**-153 392**	**-131 790**	**-120 286**	**62 884**	**65 096**	**69 265**	**-184 078**	**-175 196**	**-95 356**
Argentina	2 916	-4 312	-2 587	-10 788	-11 260	-10 515	-158	-372	-167	-8 031	-15 944	-13 270
Bolivia (Plurinational State of)	1 089	-1 899	-2 222	-1 696	-1 124	-700	1 086	1 169	1 204	478	-1 854	-1 718
Brazil	-54 736	-19 249	15 803	-52 170	-42 357	-38 136	2 725	2 724	2 800	-104 181	-58 882	-19 533
Chile	2 526	-317	521	-7 692	-6 194	-6 400	1 849	1 750	1 550	-3 316	-4 761	-4 328
Colombia	-11 300	-18 231	-14 424	-12 634	-5 825	-4 602	4 475	5 117	5 322	-19 459	-18 938	-13 705
Costa Rica	-784	-430	459	-2 062	-2 359	-2 778	412	435	444	-2 434	-2 353	-1 875
Dominican Republic	-3 185	-2 942	-2 477	-3 265	-3 045	-3 197	4 309	4 680	4 914	-2 141	-1 307	-760
Ecuador	-1 234	-2 455	303	-1 556	-1 745	-2 300	2 264	2 078	2 120	-526	-2 122	123
El Salvador	-4 467	-4 154	-3 759	-1 074	-1 137	-1 274	4 234	4 372	4 634	-1 307	-920	-399
Guatemala	-6 267	-5 896	-5 369	-1 408	-1 399	-1 650	6 445	7 199	7 702	-1 230	-96	684
Haiti	-3 089	-2 684	-2 459	50	46	37	2 291	2 437	2 377	-748	-202	-44
Honduras	-3 695	-3 746	-3 504	-1 322	-1 380	-1 569	3 572	3 835	3 950	-1 444	-1 291	-1 123
Mexico	-15 241	-23 694	-23 851	-33 804	-33 823	-30 413	22 915	24 301	26 245	-26 131	-33 216	-28 019
Nicaragua	-2 049	-2 252	-2 426	-314	-342	-344	1 450	1 548	1 595	-913	-1 045	-1 175
Panama	-3 036	328	1 518	-2 630	-3 599	-4 364	122	-106	-238	-5 544	-3 377	-3 084
Paraguay	804	337	1 329	-1 383	-1 297	-1 477	606	672	740	27	-287	592
Peru	-3 240	-4 882	-1 829	-9 328	-7 659	-9 145	4 372	3 331	3 950	-8 196	-9 210	-7 023
Uruguay	-770	130	639	-1 941	-1 495	-1 459	131	124	123	-2 580	-1 241	-697
Venezuela (Bolivarian Republic of)	12 191	-12 155	...	-8 375	-5 798	...	-218	-197	...	3 598	-18 150	...
The Caribbean	**-4 065**	**-4 977**	**...**	**-3 676**	**-1 945**	**...**	**2 970**	**2 933**	**...**	**-4 771**	**-3 989**	**...**
Antigua and Barbuda	-152	-68	-68	-36	-31	-37	28	29	29	-159	-71	-75
Bahamas	-1 490	-960	...	-438	-402	...	0	-46	...	-1 928	-1 409	...
Barbados	-219	-104	...	-197	-213	...	-14	2	...	-431	-315	...
Belize	-67	-149	...	-143	-95	...	74	70	...	-136	-175	...
Dominica	-61	-53	-70	-17	-17	-17	21	28	28	-57	-43	-60
Grenada	-170	-180	-184	-33	-34	-35	22	16	17	-181	-198	-203
Guyana	-869	-585	...	27	25	...	458	417	0	-385	-144	0
Jamaica	-3 051	-2 253	-2 358	-298	-449	-315	2 236	2 306	2 370	-1 114	-395	116
Saint Kitts and Nevis	-51	-151	-154	-26	-25	-26	42	39	37	-35	-137	-143
Saint Lucia	-111	-26	-6	-23	-22	-20	11	11	11	-123	-37	-16
Saint Vincent and the Grenadines	-226	-197	-196	0	-3	-5	44	44	45	-182	-156	-156
Suriname	-417	-846	...	-69	-27	...	71	65	...	-415	-808	...
Trinidad and Tobago	2 820	595	...	-2 421	-650	...	-21	-47	...	378	-101	...

Table A1.5 (concluded)

	Capital and financial balance[c]			Overall balance			Reserve assets (variation)[d]			Other financing		
	2014	2015	2016[a]	2014	2015	2016[a]	2014	2015	2016[a]	2014	2015	2016[a]
Latin America and the Caribbean	**219 328**	**150 938**	**...**	**37 907**	**-26 345**	**...**	**-40 175**	**23 780**	**...**	**2 272**	**2 534**	**...**
Latin America[b]	**215 720**	**148 249**	**119 961**	**35 568**	**-24 987**	**12 635**	**-37 803**	**22 494**	**-27 213**	**2 233**	**2 491**	**0**
Argentina	9 226	11 073	25 239	1 195	-4 871	0	-3 428	2 063	-11 970	2 232	2 808	0
Bolivia (Plurinational State of)	454	233	-565	932	-1 620	-2 283	-932	1 620	0	0	0	0
Brazil	115 014	60 451	27 633	10 833	1 569	8 100	-10 833	-1 569	-8 100	0	0	0
Chile	4 373	4 973	5 438	1 057	211	1 109	-1 057	-211	-1 109	0	0	0
Colombia	23 896	19 354	13 939	4 437	415	234	-4 437	-415	-234	0	0	0
Costa Rica	2 321	2 997	1 722	-113	644	-153	113	-644	153	0	0	0
Dominican Republic	2 789	2 077	435	648	770	-326	-195	-407	0	-455	-365	0
Ecuador	101	633	1 739	-424	-1 489	1 862	411	1 453	-1 862	13	36	0
El Salvador	1 274	1 033	1 063	-33	113	664	33	-113	-664	0	0	0
Guatemala	-2 292	-1 512	580	73	475	1 264	-73	-475	-1 264	0	0	0
Haiti	288	85	252	-94	-157	208	479	155	-208	-385	2	0
Honduras	1 904	1 584	1 246	459	293	122	-459	-303	-122	-1	10	0
Mexico	42 459	17 549	30 162	16 329	-15 667	2 142	-16 329	15 667	-2 142	0	0	0
Nicaragua	1 195	1 242	1 074	282	197	-101	-282	-197	101	0	0	0
Panama	5 941	3 377	3 514	397	-78	430	-1 222	78	-430	825	0	0
Paraguay	1 112	-272	131	1 138	-560	724	-1 131	560	-724	-7	0	0
Peru	6 041	9 288	7 322	-2 188	73	299	2 178	-73	-299	10	0	0
Uruguay	3 940	-547	-963	1 360	-1 788	-1 660	-1 360	1 788	1 660	0	0	0
Venezuela (Bolivarian Republic of)	-4 316	14 632	...	-718	-3 518	...	718	3 518	...	0	0	...
The Caribbean	**3 608**	**2 689**	**...**	**2 339**	**-1 358**	**...**	**-2 372**	**1 286**	**...**	**38**	**43**	**...**
Antigua and Barbuda	253	128	75	94	58	0	-94	-59	0	0	0	0
Bahamas	1 974	1 433	...	46	24	0	-46	-24	...	2	0	...
Barbados	386	252	...	-46	-63	...	46	63	...	0	0	...
Belize	221	71	...	85	-104	...	-84	104	...	-1	0	...
Dominica	75	65	60	18	21	0	-15	-26	0	0	0	0
Grenada	204	228	203	23	30	0	-23	-30	0	0	0	0
Guyana	408	169	...	22	25	...	-59	-68	0	37	43	...
Jamaica	-1 588	882	520	800	428	-197	-800	-428	197	0	0	0
Saint Kitts and Nevis	62	99	143	27	-38	0	-27	38	0	0	0	0
Saint Lucia	190	76	16	67	39	0	-67	-63	0	0	0	0
Saint Vincent and the Grenadines	205	171	156	23	15	0	-23	-15	0	0	0	0
Suriname	265	542	...	-150	-266	...	150	266	...	0	0	...
Trinidad and Tobago	952	-1 427	...	1 330	-1 529	...	-1 330	1 529	...	0	0	...

Source: Economic Commission for Latin America and the Caribbean (ECLAC), on the basis of official figures.

[a] Estimates.
[b] Does not include the Bolivarian Republic of Venezuela.
[c] Includes errors and omissions.
[d] A minus sign (-) indicates an increase in reserve assets.

Table A1.6
Latin America and the Caribbean: international trade of goods
(Indices: 2010=100)

| | Exports of goods, f.o.b. | | | | | | Unit value | | |
| | Value | | | Volume | | | | | |
	2014	2015	2016[a]	2014	2015	2016[a]	2014	2015	2016[a]
Latin America	**120.5**	**103.0**	**98.0**	**112.5**	**115.3**	**116.2**	**107.2**	**89.4**	**84.4**
Argentina	100.3	83.3	83.8	85.6	84.1	90.0	117.3	99.0	93.1
Bolivia (Plurinational State of)	200.1	135.5	109.7	151.9	129.8	119.5	131.7	104.4	91.9
Brazil	111.3	94.4	91.1	103.7	112.1	116.3	107.4	84.2	78.3
Chile	96.8	80.4	76.0	102.6	100.5	102.1	94.3	80.0	74.4
Colombia	139.6	93.5	79.5	139.4	143.1	139.8	100.1	65.4	56.9
Costa Rica	126.7	125.5	133.0	126.3	131.7	138.2	100.3	95.3	96.3
Dominican Republic	145.3	139.7	137.0	143.7	148.6	147.1	101.1	94.0	93.1
Ecuador	146.6	105.0	92.4	125.5	125.2	126.6	116.8	83.9	73.0
El Salvador	122.5	126.1	122.3	110.3	112.2	108.8	111.0	112.5	112.5
Guatemala	128.8	126.8	123.0	129.3	135.5	136.9	99.6	93.6	89.9
Haiti	170.6	181.8	177.7	156.9	166.2	163.9	108.7	109.3	108.4
Honduras	128.9	128.4	123.9	130.2	135.1	137.3	98.9	95.0	90.2
Mexico	133.1	127.5	123.7	125.2	130.8	131.5	106.3	97.5	94.1
Nicaragua	149.4	137.8	130.9	135.8	129.0	127.6	110.0	106.8	102.6
Panama	118.1	100.9	86.7	110.5	95.6	84.8	106.9	105.4	102.3
Paraguay	125.1	104.0	107.2	112.3	100.4	108.9	111.4	103.6	98.4
Peru	110.4	95.6	98.6	105.8	107.6	116.6	104.4	88.8	84.6
Uruguay	128.8	113.0	104.1	108.2	106.9	104.8	119.0	105.7	99.4
Venezuela (Bolivarian Republic of)	111.7	55.9	39.2	92.0	83.7	70.3	121.4	66.8	55.7

| | Imports of goods, f.o.b. | | | | | | Unit value | | |
| | Value | | | Volume | | | | | |
	2014	2015	2016[a]	2014	2015	2016[a]	2014	2015	2016[a]
Latin America	**127.6**	**113.7**	**103.4**	**116.3**	**112.5**	**107.6**	**109.7**	**101.1**	**96.1**
Argentina	115.3	105.6	98.8	103.6	107.5	111.8	111.3	98.2	88.4
Bolivia (Plurinational State of)	176.9	161.1	138.5	107.3	100.3	92.7	164.9	160.6	149.3
Brazil	126.2	94.3	76.4	112.9	95.7	84.3	111.8	98.5	90.6
Chile	94.1	80.6	75.8	89.9	86.9	86.4	104.7	92.8	87.7
Colombia	160.2	135.5	114.4	146.6	143.4	131.5	109.3	94.5	87.0
Costa Rica	133.9	131.0	133.6	129.4	140.6	146.4	103.5	93.1	91.3
Dominican Republic	113.6	110.9	110.3	104.8	119.0	123.3	108.4	93.2	89.5
Ecuador	135.7	105.4	80.1	123.9	100.4	79.5	109.5	104.9	100.7
El Salvador	126.3	124.3	116.9	113.3	123.1	120.5	111.4	101.0	97.0
Guatemala	133.2	127.9	121.5	123.5	131.7	131.7	107.9	97.1	92.2
Haiti	121.8	114.5	107.1	93.1	97.7	94.7	130.9	117.1	113.0
Honduras	124.3	124.6	119.6	113.6	125.0	127.6	109.4	99.7	93.7
Mexico	132.7	131.1	127.9	121.8	124.6	125.3	108.9	105.2	102.1
Nicaragua	138.5	139.8	142.6	126.0	146.2	158.6	109.9	95.6	89.9
Panama	149.8	130.6	115.0	139.7	128.3	117.0	107.2	101.8	98.3
Paraguay	125.9	107.5	101.1	116.7	111.5	112.7	107.9	96.4	89.7
Peru	142.4	129.7	124.0	127.7	128.1	125.8	111.5	101.3	98.6
Uruguay	131.5	109.1	95.0	124.1	118.2	113.0	105.9	92.4	84.0
Venezuela (Bolivarian Republic of)	113.8	88.4	52.6	104.9	87.6	54.3	108.5	101.0	96.9

Source: Economic Commission for Latin America and the Caribbean (ECLAC), on the basis of official figures.
[a] Estimates.

Table A1.7
Latin America: terms of trade for goods f.o.b./f.o.b.
(Indices: 2010=100)

	2007	2008	2009	2010	2011	2012	2013	2014	2015	2016[a]
Latin America	**93.9**	**97.1**	**89.5**	**100.0**	**108.0**	**104.5**	**102.3**	**97.7**	**88.4**	**87.8**
Argentina	85.5	95.9	96.6	100.0	110.9	115.7	108.1	105.4	100.8	105.3
Bolivia (Plurinational State of)	93.9	99.0	95.2	100.0	118.1	112.3	94.5	79.9	65.0	61.5
Brazil	85.3	88.5	86.2	100.0	107.8	101.5	99.4	96.1	85.5	86.4
Chile	91.7	78.4	82.0	100.0	101.3	94.8	91.9	90.1	86.2	84.8
Colombia	86.2	91.3	86.1	100.0	114.6	108.2	100.5	91.6	69.1	65.4
Costa Rica	104.7	100.8	104.1	100.0	96.3	95.8	96.1	97.0	102.3	105.5
Dominican Republic	100.5	96.0	103.8	100.0	94.7	93.8	91.5	93.3	100.9	104.0
Ecuador	...	...	...	100.0	112.4	112.1	113.2	106.7	80.0	72.5
El Salvador	104.0	94.1	105.9	100.0	97.5	98.0	96.3	99.6	111.3	116.0
Guatemala	95.1	92.6	100.5	100.0	99.1	93.7	91.8	92.3	96.4	97.4
Haiti	111.2	79.9	103.4	100.0	83.0	86.0	80.6	83.1	93.4	95.9
Honduras	97.0	91.1	97.3	100.0	108.4	94.6	88.6	90.4	95.3	96.3
Mexico	103.3	104.6	92.9	100.0	106.8	102.9	102.8	97.6	92.6	92.2
Nicaragua	94.6	90.9	97.9	100.0	106.6	106.5	98.2	100.1	111.7	114.1
Panama	101.9	97.3	101.9	100.0	97.8	98.2	97.7	99.7	103.5	104.1
Paraguay	95.3	102.3	100.0	100.0	102.4	103.4	102.8	103.3	107.5	109.8
Peru	95.0	84.6	82.6	100.0	107.2	105.0	99.0	93.6	87.7	85.8
Uruguay	87.1	94.1	100.5	100.0	102.4	106.3	108.1	112.3	114.5	118.2
Venezuela (Bolivarian Republic of)	93.6	115.5	84.1	100.0	120.2	121.4	118.9	111.8	66.1	57.5

Source: Economic Commission for Latin America and the Caribbean (ECLAC), on the basis of official figures.
[a] Estimates.

Table A1.8
Latin America and the Caribbean (selected countries): remittances from emigrant workers
(Millions of dollars)

	2007	2008	2009	2010	2011	2012	2013	2014	2015	2016[a]
Bolivia (Plurinational State of)	1 020	1 097	1 023	939	1 012	1 094	1 182	1 164	1 179	792[b]
Brazil[c]	2 809	2 913	2 224	2 518	2 550	2 191	2 124	2 128	2 459	1 576[b]
Colombia	4 430	4 785	4 090	3 996	4 064	3 970	4 401	4 093	4 635	3 942
Costa Rica	596	584	489	505	487	527	561	559	518	249[d]
Dominican Republic[c]	...	...	...	3 683	4 008	4 045	4 262	4 571	4 961	3 949[e]
Ecuador[c]	3 335	3 083	2 736	2 591	2 672	2 467	2 450	2 462	2 378	1 264[d]
El Salvador	3 695	3 742	3 387	3 455	3 628	3 880	3 938	4 133	4 270	3 728
Guatemala	4 128	4 315	3 912	4 127	4 378	4 783	5 105	5 544	6 285	5 881
Haiti	2 510	2 707	2 403	2 526	2 750	2 842	3 093	3 437	3 726	2 924[e]
Honduras	1 964	2 021	1 792	1 906	2 025	2 037	2 065	2 157	2 226	1 125[d]
Jamaica	26 059	25 145	21 306	21 304	22 803	22 438	22 303	23 647	24 792	20 045[e]
Mexico	740	818	768	823	912	1 014	1 078	1 136	1 193	922[e]
Nicaragua	198	202	201	274	451	528	519	422	462	387[e]
Peru	2 131	2 444	2 409	2 534	2 697	2 788	2 707	2 637	2 725	1 393[d]

Source: Economic Commission for Latin America and the Caribbean (ECLAC), on the basis of official figures.
[a] Figures as of October.
[b] Figures as of August.
[c] New methodology according to the sixth edition of the Balance of Payments Manual of the International Monetary Fund (IMF).
[d] Figures as of June.
[e] Figures as of September.

Table A1.9
Latin America and the Caribbean: net resource transfer[a]
(Millions of dollars)

	2007	2008	2009	2010	2011	2012	2013	2014	2015	2016[b]
Latin America and the Caribbean	43 751	-46 263	-16 201	36 195	43 628	27 986	23 333	64 531	19 737	392
Latin America[c]	45 418	-43 876	-15 174	39 973	45 708	26 861	26 900	64 561	18 950	-325
Argentina	-198	-10 991	-14 023	-14 284	-10 809	-14 397	-10 054	670	2 621	14 724
Bolivia (Plurinational State of)	-128	-177	-1 094	-707	923	-1 888	-1 840	-1 242	-891	-1 265
Brazil	56 642	-9 401	37 269	57 870	65 194	38 810	36 374	62 844	18 094	-10 503
Chile	-1 352	-15 786	-9 657	-914	218	-4 033	115	-3 318	-1 222	-962
Colombia	2 945	-517	-2 257	588	-2 018	1 626	4 882	11 262	13 529	9 336
Costa Rica	1 929	2 022	-180	589	979	3 065	1 064	258	639	-1 056
Cuba	-960	...	...	...	...	...	...	...	...	...
Dominican Republic	665	2 462	1 248	3 167	2 522	1 079	686	-931	-1 333	-2 762
Ecuador	-2 760	-2 418	-1 883	-625	-522	-1 611	1 427	-1 441	-1 076	-561
El Salvador	1 039	1 477	179	-302	79	1 039	267	200	-104	-211
Guatemala	1 159	-2 022	-1 172	-3 026	-3 740	-3 831	-4 250	-3 699	-2 911	-1 070
Haiti	688	374	373	971	573	788	1 022	-47	133	290
Honduras	612	1 531	-429	546	521	33	894	581	214	-324
Mexico	2 423	8 201	-1 921	12 579	21 204	8 679	8 028	8 655	-16 274	-251
Nicaragua	1 124	1 316	895	761	993	777	948	881	901	730
Panama	712	1 732	-664	1 223	2 854	673	1 585	4 136	-222	-850
Paraguay	-1 046	-915	-767	-1 036	-603	-1 184	-1 127	-279	-1 569	-1 346
Peru	-95	-219	-6 684	3 557	-5 455	7 573	879	-3 277	1 629	-1 823
Uruguay	710	3 045	929	-1 131	2 248	4 344	3 903	1 999	-2 042	-2 422
Venezuela (Bolivarian Republic of)	-18 691	-23 589	-15 337	-19 853	-29 453	-14 681	-17 901	-12 691	8 834	...
The Caribbean	-1 667	-2 387	-1 027	-3 779	-2 080	1 126	-3 568	-30	787	717
Antigua and Barbuda	333	292	108	146	88	140	191	217	97	38
Bahamas	723	903	909	627	992	1 162	1 096	1 538	1 031	...
Barbados	233	136	182	116	254	251	45	188	39	...
Belize	-84	38	22	-107	-60	-32	68	77	-24	...
Dominica	66	108	118	70	67	81	23	58	47	43
Grenada	211	201	160	154	177	157	223	171	194	168
Guyana	137	262	-51	101	341	311	568	471	236	...
Jamaica	937	2 120	430	91	1 277	86	-1 171	-1 886	432	205
Saint Kitts and Nevis	89	183	172	142	129	52	50	36	74	117
Saint Lucia	295	257	125	195	231	158	84	167	54	-5
Saint Vincent and the Grenadines	168	204	189	221	163	208	247	205	168	151
Suriname	-181	-96	-68	-720	-569	-175	-84	196	514	...
Trinidad and Tobago	-4 594	-6 995	-3 324	-4 816	-5 170	-1 273	-4 909	-1 469	-2 077	...

Source: Economic Commission for Latin America and the Caribbean (ECLAC), on the basis of official figures.

[a] The net resource transfer is calculated as total net capital income minus the income balance (net payments of profits and interest). Total net capital income is the balance on the capital and financial accounts plus errors and omissions, plus loans and the use of IMF credit plus exceptional financing. Negative figures indicate resources transferred outside the country.
[b] Preliminary figures.
[c] Does not include the Bolivarian Republic of Venezuela.

Table A1.10
Latin America and the Caribbean: net foreign direct investment[a]
(Millions of dollars)

	2007	2008	2009	2010	2011	2012	2013	2014	2015	2016
Latin America and the Caribbean	96 000	103 021	72 157	110 405	153 484	148 447	142 086	142 354	134 795	...
Latin America	92 007	97 049	69 028	107 487	150 927	146 205	141 250	139 605	133 750	...
Argentina	4 969	8 335	3 306	10 368	9 352	14 269	8 932	3 145	11 103	...
Bolivia (Plurinational State of)	362	508	426	672	859	1 060	1 750	690	495	...
Brazil	27 518	24 601	36 033	61 689	85 091	81 399	54 240	70 855	61 576	...
Chile	7 453	7 137	4 730	3 916	9 491	7 126	7 117	9 428	4 663	...
Colombia	7 607	7 480	4 530	947	6 228	15 646	8 557	12 426	7 514	...
Costa Rica	1 634	2 072	1 340	1 589	2 328	1 803	2 401	2 553	2 542	...
Dominican Republic	1 667	2 870	2 165	1 622	2 277	3 142	1 990	2 032	2 199	...
Ecuador	627	558	683	165	644	567	727	772	1 321	...
El Salvador	1 455	824	366	-226	218	484	176	311	429	...
Guatemala	720	770	626	829	1 043	1 284	1 329	1 495	1 338	...
Haiti	75	30	55	178	119	156	162	99	106	...
Honduras	926	1 007	505	971	1 012	851	992	1 120	1 113	...
Mexico	24 201	28 224	8 527	12 094	11 685	-2 293	34 199	20 282	22 127	...
Nicaragua	366	608	463	474	929	703	700	804	785	...
Panama	1 777	2 196	1 259	2 363	2 956	3 254	3 612	3 980	4 586	...
Paraguay	202	209	95	216	557	697	252	382	260	...
Peru	5 425	6 188	6 020	8 189	7 518	11 840	9 161	7 789	7 690	...
Uruguay	1 240	2 117	1 512	2 349	2 511	2 539	3 027	2 148	1 293	...
Venezuela (Bolivarian Republic of)	3 783	1 316	-3 613	-918	6 110	1 679	1 928	-704	2 609	...
The Caribbean	3 992	5 972	3 129	2 918	2 557	2 242	836	2 749	1 045	...
Antigua and Barbuda	338	159	81	97	65	133	95	149	148	...
Bahamas	746	860	664	872	667	530	388	251	76	...
Barbados	559	689	484	747	758	186	46	791	335	...
Belize	139	167	108	95	95	193	92	138	59	...
Dominica	40	57	42	43	35	59	23	33	34	...
Grenada	157	135	103	60	43	31	113	38	60	...
Guyana	152	178	164	198	247	278	201	238	117	...
Jamaica	751	1 361	480	169	144	-411	-631	-584	-931	...
Saint Kitts and Nevis	134	178	131	116	110	108	136	118	76	...
Saint Lucia	272	161	146	121	81	74	92	91	93	...
Saint Vincent and the Grenadines	119	159	110	97	86	115	160	109	120	...
Suriname	-247	-231	-93	-248	73	173	188	163	276	...
Trinidad and Tobago	830	2 101	709	549	156	772	-66	1 214	583	...

Source: Economic Commission for Latin America and the Caribbean (ECLAC), on the basis of official figures.
[a] Corresponds to direct investment in the reporting economy after deduction of outward direct investment by residents of that country. Includes reinvestment of profits.

Table A1.11
Latin America and the Caribbean: gross external debt[a]
(Millions of dollars, end-of-period stocks)

		2007	2008	2009	2010	2011	2012	2013	2014	2015	2016[a]
Latin America and the Caribbean[b]		**738 254**	**769 247**	**834 876**	**999 251**	**1 123 667**	**1 235 162**	**1 300 637**	**1 421 974**	**1 457 798**	**1 542 753**
Latin America		**725 174**	**755 688**	**820 515**	**982 308**	**1 105 723**	**1 217 197**	**1 281 411**	**1 401 701**	**1 435 937**	**1 519 411**
Argentina	Total	125 366	125 859	119 267	134 011	145 154	145 722	141 491	144 801	152 632	188 266
Bolivia (Plurinational State of)	Total	5 403	5 930	5 801	5 875	6 298	6 625	7 756	8 543	9 445	9 941
Brazil	Total	193 159	198 492	198 136	256 804	298 204	327 590	312 517	352 684	334 745	335 361
Chile	Total	53 627	63 534	72 617	84 986	99 306	120 446	134 550	149 652	155 656	162 588
Colombia	Total	44 553	46 369	53 719	64 738	75 568	78 763	91 976	101 282	110 596	116 378
Costa Rica	Total	8 075	8 827	8 276	9 527	11 286	15 381	19 629	21 671	23 903	25 389
Dominican Republic	Public	6 556	7 219	8 215	9 947	11 625	12 872	14 919	16 074	16 029	17 162
Ecuador	Total	17 445	16 900	13 514	13 914	15 210	15 913	18 788	24 112	27 193	32 725
El Salvador	Total	9 349	9 994	9 882	9 698	10 670	12 521	13 238	14 885	15 482	15 908
Guatemala	Total	10 909	11 163	11 248	12 026	14 021	15 339	17 307	19 530	20 385	20 775
Haiti	Public	1 627	1 921	1 333	354	709	1 173	1 562	1 875	1 985	...
Honduras	Total	3 190	3 499	3 365	3 785	4 208	4 861	6 709	7 184	7 462	7 337
Mexico	Total	124 995	123 626	160 427	193 971	209 766	225 973	259 535	285 754	297 896	321 153
Nicaragua	Public	3 385	3 512	3 661	4 068	4 263	4 481	4 724	4 796	4 804	5 000
Panama	Public	8 276	8 477	10 150	10 439	10 858	10 782	12 231	14 352	15 648	16 689
Paraguay	Total	2 731	3 220	3 177	3 713	3 970	4 563	4 776	6 126	6 513	7 083
Peru	Total	33 239	34 997	35 157	43 674	47 977	59 376	60 823	64 512	68 244	69 746
Uruguay	Total	14 864	15 425	17 969	18 425	18 345	24 030	26 518	28 100	28 451	27 057
Venezuela (Bolivarian Republic of)	Total	58 426	66 727	84 602	102 354	118 285	130 785	132 362	135 767	138 869	...
The Caribbean	**Public**	**13 081**	**13 559**	**14 361**	**16 943**	**17 945**	**17 965**	**19 226**	**20 273**	**21 861**	**23 342**
Antigua and Barbuda	Public	481	436	416	432	467	445	577	560	570	622
Bahamas	Public	337	443	767	916	1 045	1 465	1 616	2 095	2 100	2 294
Barbados	Public	1 103	1 089	1 321	1 523	1 564	1 490	1 590	1 652	1 610	1 579
Belize	Public	973	958	1 017	1 021	1 032	1 029	1 083	1 127	1 177	1 192
Dominica	Public	241	234	222	232	238	263	273	278	281	274
Grenada	Public	469	481	512	528	535	535	562	578	581	605
Guyana	Public	718	834	933	1 043	1 206	1 358	1 246	1 216	1 143	1 140
Jamaica	Public	6 123	6 344	6 594	8 390	8 626	8 256	8 310	8 659	10 314	10 225
Saint Kitts and Nevis	Public	323	312	325	296	320	317	320	280	210	199
Saint Lucia	Public	399	364	373	393	417	435	488	526	457	568
Saint Vincent and the Grenadines	Public	219	229	262	313	328	329	354	385	378	351
Suriname	Public	298	319	269	334	463	567	739	810	876	1 042
Trinidad and Tobago	Public	1 398	1 515	1 351	1 522	1 706	1 478	2 068	2 109	2 164	3 251

Source: Economic Commission for Latin America and the Caribbean (ECLAC), on the basis of official figures.
[a] Preliminary figures.
[b] Includes debt owed to the International Monetary Fund.

Table A1.12
Latin America and the Caribbean: sovereign spreads on EMBI+ and EMBI global
(Basis points to end of period)

		2007	2008	2009	2010	2011	2012	2013	2014	2015	2016[a]
Latin America	**EMBI+**	**268**	**722**	**328**	**305**	**410**	**317**	**410**	**491**	**584**	**476**
Argentina	EMBI+	410	1 704	660	496	925	991	808	719	438	451
Belize	EMBI Global	...	...	...	617	1 391	2 245	807	819	822	1 284
Bolivia (Plurinational State of)	EMBI Global	...	...	...	...	...	...	289	277	250	130
Brazil	EMBI+	221	428	192	189	223	142	224	259	523	313
Chile	EMBI Global	151	343	95	115	172	116	148	169	253	177
Colombia	EMBI+	195	498	196	172	195	112	166	196	321	239
Dominican Republic	EMBI Global	...	...	...	322	597	343	349	381	421	386
Ecuador	EMBI Global	614	4 731	769	913	846	826	530	883	1 266	743
El Salvador	EMBI Global	...	...	...	302	478	396	389	414	634	478
Jamaica	EMBI Global	...	...	...	427	637	711	641	485	469	386
Mexico	EMBI+	149	376	164	149	187	126	155	182	232	220
Panama	EMBI+	184	540	171	162	201	129	199	189	218	168
Paraguay	EMBI Global	...	...	...	...	...	...	240	291	338	268
Peru	EMBI+	178	509	165	163	216	114	159	181	246	163
Uruguay	EMBI Global	243	685	238	188	213	127	194	208	280	230
Venezuela (Bolivarian Republic of)	EMBI+	506	1 862	1 017	1 044	1 197	773	1 093	2 295	2 658	2 281

Source: Economic Commission for Latin America and the Caribbean (ECLAC), on the basis of information from JPMorgan, Emerging Markets Bond Index Monitor.
[a] Figures as of October.

Table A1.13
Latin America and the Caribbean: sovereign risk premiums on five-year credit default swaps
(Basis points to end of period)

	2007	2008	2009	2010	2011	2012	2013	2014	2015	2016[a]
Argentina	462	4 041	914	602	922	1 442	1 654	2 987	5 393	446
Brazil	103	301	123	111	162	108	194	201	495	297
Chile	32	203	68	84	132	72	80	94	129	89
Colombia	130	309	143	113	156	96	119	141	243	191
Mexico	69	293	134	114	154	98	92	103	170	181
Panama	118	302	134	99	150	98	111	109	182	138
Peru	116	304	124	113	172	97	133	115	188	119
Venezuela (Bolivarian Republic of)	452	3 218	1 104	1 016	928	647	1 150	3 155	4 868	4 079

Source: Economic Commission for Latin America and the Caribbean (ECLAC), on the basis of information from Bloomberg.
[a] Figures as of October.

Table A1.14
Latin America and the Caribbean: international bond issues[a]
(Millions of dollars)

	2007	2008	2009	2010	2011	2012	2013	2014	2015	2016[b]
Total	41 515	19 848	64 750	90 183	91 687	114 241	123 332	133 056	78 606	116 713
National issues	40 976	19 401	63 250	88 657	90 272	111 757	121 518	129 743	75 436	111 933
Argentina	3 256	65	500	3 146	2 449	663	1 025	1 941	3 586	33 083
Bahamas	-	100	300	-	-	-	-	300	-	-
Barbados	-	-	450	390	-	-	-	2 500	320	-
Bolivia (Plurinational State of)	-	-	-	-	-	500	500	-	-	-
Brazil	10 608	6 520	25 745	39 305	38 369	50 255	37 262	45 364	7 188	20 481
Chile	250	-	2 773	6 750	6 049	9 443	11 540	13 768	7 650	4 692
Colombia	3 065	1 000	5 450	1 912	6 411	7 459	10 012	9 200	6 400	4 061
Costa Rica	-	-	-	-	250	1 250	3 000	1 000	1 000	500
Dominican Republic	605	-	-	1 034	750	750	1 800	1 500	3 500	1 870
Ecuador	-	-	-	-	-	-	-	2 000	1 500	2 000
El Salvador	-	-	800	450	654	800	310	800	300	-
Guatemala	-	30	-	-	150	1 400	1 300	1 100	-	700
Honduras	-	-	-	20	-	-	1 000	-	-	-
Jamaica	1 900	350	750	1 075	694	1 750	1 800	1 800	2 925	364
Mexico	10 296	6 000	16 659	26 882	22 276	28 147	41 729	37 592	30 075	36 039
Panama	670	686	1 323	-	897	1 100	1 350	1 935	1 700	2 200
Paraguay	-	-	-	-	100	500	500	1 000	280	600
Peru	1 827	-	2 150	4 693	2 155	7 240	5 840	5 944	6 407	1 960
Suriname	-	-	-	-	-	-	-	-	-	636
Trinidad and Tobago	-	-	850	-	175	-	550	-	-	1 600
Uruguay	999	-	500	-	1 693	500	2 000	2 000	2 605	1 147
Venezuela (Bolivarian Republic of)	7 500	4 650	5 000	3 000	7 200	-	-	-	-	-
Supranational issues	539	447	1 500	1 526	1 415	2 484	1 814	3 313	3 171	4 780
Central American Bank for Economic Integration (CABEI)	-	-	500	151	-	250	520	505	521	831
Caribbean Development Bank (CDB)	-	-	-	-	175	-	-	-	-	-
Foreign Trade Bank of Latin America (BLADEX)	-	-	-	-	-	400	-	-	-	73
Development Bank of Latin America (CAF)	539	447	1 000	1 375	1 240	1 834	1 294	2 808	2 650	3 376
Inter-American Investment Corporation	-	-	-	-	-	-	-	-	-	500

Source: Economic Commission for Latin America and the Caribbean (ECLAC), on the basis of information from Merrill Lynch, J.P. Morgan and Latin Finance.
[a] Includes sovereign, bank and corporate bonds.
[b] Figures as of October.

Table A1.15
Latin America and the Caribbean: stock exchange indices
(National indices to end of period. 31 December 2005=100)

	2007	2008	2009	2010	2011	2012	2013	2014	2015	2016[a]
Argentina	139	70	150	228	160	185	349	556	757	1 130
Brazil	191	112	205	207	170	182	154	149	130	185
Chile	155	121	182	251	213	219	188	196	187	214
Colombia	112	79	122	163	133	155	137	122	90	101
Costa Rica	217	207	142	118	121	129	190	211	191	252
Ecuador	121	128	107	126	128	135	148	168	161	148
Jamaica	103	77	80	82	91	88	77	73	144	171
Mexico	166	126	180	217	208	246	240	242	241	255
Peru	365	147	295	487	406	430	328	308	205	321
Trinidad and Tobago	92	79	72	78	95	100	111	108	109	113
Venezuela (Bolivarian Republic of)	186	172	270	320	574	2 312	13 421	18 925	71 546	162 829

Source: Economic Commission for Latin America and the Caribbean (ECLAC), on the basis of information from Bloomberg.
[a] Figures as of November.

Table A1.16
Latin America and the Caribbean: gross international reserves
(Millions of dollars, end-of-period stocks)

	2007	2008	2009	2010	2011	2012	2013	2014	2015	2016[a]
Latin America and the Caribbean	**459 581**	**512 727**	**567 444**	**655 305**	**773 632**	**835 735**	**830 018**	**857 438**	**811 762**	**829 202**
Latin America	**448 480**	**498 906**	**553 531**	**639 428**	**756 688**	**820 026**	**813 984**	**839 356**	**795 043**	**812 196**
Argentina	45 711	46 198	47 967	52 145	46 376	43 290	30 599	31 443	25 563	37 210[b]
Bolivia (Plurinational State of)	5 319	7 722	8 580	9 730	12 019	13 927	14 430	15 123	13 056	10 694[b]
Brazil	180 334	193 783	238 520	288 575	352 012	373 147	358 808	363 551	356 464	365 556
Chile	16 910	23 162	25 373	27 864	41 979	41 650	41 094	40 447	38 643	39 468
Colombia	20 955	24 041	25 365	28 464	32 303	37 474	43 639	47 328	46 740	46 974[b]
Costa Rica	4 114	3 799	4 066	4 627	4 756	6 857	7 331	7 211	7 834	7 556
Dominican Republic	2 946	2 662	3 307	3 765	4 098	3 559	4 701	4 862	5 266	5 453[b]
Ecuador[c]	3 521	4 473	3 792	2 622	2 958	2 483	4 361	3 949	2 496	4 275[b]
El Salvador	2 197	2 544	2 985	2 882	2 503	3 175	2 745	2 693	2 787	3 294[b]
Guatemala	4 320	4 659	5 213	5 954	6 188	6 694	7 273	7 333	7 751	9 063[b]
Haiti	494	587	733	1 284	1 344	1 337	1 690	1 163	977	1 034[d]
Honduras	2 733	2 690	2 174	2 775	2 880	2 629	3 113	3 570	3 874	3 926[e]
Mexico	87 211	95 302	99 893	120 587	149 209	167 050	180 200	195 682	177 597	176 852[b]
Nicaragua	1 032	1 062	1 490	1 708	1 793	1 778	1 874	2 147	2 353	2 210
Panama	2 094	2 637	3 222	2 561	2 234	2 441	2 775	3 994	3 911	4 109[e]
Paraguay	2 462	2 864	3 861	4 168	4 984	4 994	5 871	6 891	6 200	6 924[b]
Peru	27 720	31 233	33 175	44 150	48 859	64 049	65 710	62 353	61 537	62 049[b]
Uruguay	4 121	6 360	7 987	7 656	10 302	13 605	16 290	17 555	15 634	13 800
Venezuela (Bolivarian Republic of)	34 286	43 127	35 830	27 911	29 892	29 890	21 481	22 061	16 361	11 748
The Caribbean	**11 101**	**13 821**	**13 913**	**15 877**	**16 944**	**15 709**	**16 034**	**18 081**	**16 718**	**17 007**
Antigua and Barbuda[c]	144	138	108	136	147	161	202	297	356	410[d]
Bahamas	454	563	816	861	892	812	740	787	808	903[b]
Barbados	622	523	563	575	587	630	516	467	434	415[b]
Belize	99	156	210	216	242	289	402	483	432	361[b]
Dominica[c]	60	55	64	66	75	92	85	100	125	157[d]
Grenada[c]	110	104	112	103	106	104	135	158	189	195[d]
Guyana	313	356	628	780	798	862	777	666	599	610[e]
Jamaica	1 906	1 795	1 752	2 979	2 820	1 981	1 818	2 473	2 914	3 027[b]
Saint Kitts and Nevis[c]	96	110	123	157	233	252	291	318	280	343[d]
Saint Lucia[c]	151	140	151	184	192	208	168	235	298	311[d]
Saint Vincent and the Grenadines[c]	86	83	75	111	88	109	133	156	165	169[d]
Suriname	401	433	659	639	941	1 008	779	625	330	350[e]
Trinidad and Tobago	6 659	9 364	8 652	9 070	9 823	9 201	9 987	11 317	9 788	9 757[b]

Source: Economic Commission for Latin America and the Caribbean (ECLAC), on the basis of official figures.
[a] Figures as of November.
[b] Figures as of October.
[c] Net international reserves.
[d] Figures as of June.
[e] Figures as of September.

Table A1.17

Latin America and the Caribbean: real effective exchange rates[a] [b]

(Indices: 2005=100, average values for the period)

	2007	2008	2009	2010	2011	2012	2013	2014	2015	2016[c] [d]
Latin America and the Caribbean[e]	**95.0**	**89.9**	**90.5**	**85.5**	**83.8**	**82.2**	**81.9**	**82.7**	**83.6**	**85.2**
Barbados	98.7	97.7	93.3	89.5	90.5	89.5	89.5	89.9	89.4	88.3
Bolivia (Plurinational State of)	101.8	93.4	85.5	89.9	89.8	87.0	81.7	76.4	68.2	63.8
Brazil	82.8	80.4	82.3	72.0	69.2	77.7	83.1	85.8	106.9	104.4
Chile	97.1	97.3	101.6	96.3	95.3	94.0	95.2	105.4	108.8	109.0
Colombia	91.4	87.8	91.8	79.3	79.5	76.5	80.1	84.8	107.3	110.9
Costa Rica	97.4	94.1	92.8	82.4	79.7	76.6	74.1	77.4	73.5	74.6
Dominica	104.6	105.5	107.9	106.4	109.7	109.0	110.9	112.2	110.9	110.5
Dominican Republic	105.0	105.9	110.5	108.9	110.3	112.3	115.8	120.7	124.1	122.3
Ecuador	106.9	108.6	100.9	99.9	102.4	98.4	96.7	93.7	85.1	83.7
El Salvador	100.9	101.7	99.6	101.2	102.4	103.1	104.1	105.3	104.7	104.2
Guatemala	96.4	91.2	94.4	93.5	89.5	88.3	87.2	83.8	77.9	74.1
Honduras	97.5	94.2	87.1	86.1	85.4	83.8	84.8	82.4	81.9	83.4
Jamaica	104.9	99.2	110.8	98.2	96.3	95.3	100.0	109.4	117.9	122.0
Mexico	100.9	103.4	117.9	109.1	109.1	112.6	106.8	108.2	122.4	138.8
Nicaragua	100.4	94.9	103.4	100.8	105.8	103.4	100.1	101.9	102.4	103.8
Panama	105.8	106.5	103.5	103.0	103.9	94.4	92.3	90.6	86.2	85.1
Paraguay	82.1	73.8	81.6	80.1	71.7	73.0	68.5	66.4	67.4	69.1
Peru	102.6	99.5	97.8	94.4	96.6	90.1	90.6	92.7	94.3	96.7
Trinidad and Tobago	94.8	90.7	82.7	79.0	79.6	73.9	70.9	67.3	61.4	61.9
Uruguay	99.3	93.3	91.3	79.9	77.9	76.3	70.8	74.9	78.0	78.5
Venezuela (Bolivarian Republic of)	84.3	68.1	52.3	79.1	69.6	58.7	60.3	...	...	...

Source: Economic Commission for Latin America and the Caribbean (ECLAC), on the basis of official figures.

[a] A country's overall real effective exchange rate index is calculated by weighting its real bilateral exchange rate indices with each of its trading partners by each partner's share in the country's total trade flows in terms of exports and imports. The extraregional real effective exchange rate index excludes trade with other Latin American and Caribbean countries.

[b] Currency depreciates in real effective terms when this index rises and appreciates when it falls.

[c] Preliminary figures.

[d] Figures as of September.

[e] Simple average of the extraregional real effective exchange rate for 18 countries. Does not include countries with multiple exchange rates.

Table A1.18
Latin America and the Caribbean: participation rate
(Average annual rates)

		2007	2008	2009	2010	2011	2012	2013	2014	2015	2015	2016[a]
											January to September	
Latin America and the Caribbean[b]		**61.8**	**61.8**	**62.1**	**61.8**	**61.7**	**61.7**	**61.6**	**61.5**	**61.5**	...	...
Argentina[c]	Urban areas	59.5	58.8	59.3	58.9	59.5	59.3	58.9	58.3	57.7[d]	...	...
Bahamas	Nationwide total	...	...	73.4	...	72.3	74.6	73.2	73.7	74.3	73.0	76.9[e]
Barbados	Nationwide total	67.8	67.6	67.0	66.6	67.6	66.2	66.7	63.9	65.1	65.2	65.3[f]
Belize	Nationwide total	61.2	59.2	...	...	...	65.8	64.0	63.6	63.2	63.4	63.7[g]
Bolivia (Plurinational State of)	Nationwide total	64.8	64.9	65.1	...	65.8	61.2	63.4	65.9	...	...	...
Brazil[h]	Nationwide total[i]	56.9	57.0	56.7	57.1	57.1	61.4	61.3	61.0	61.3	61.2	61.4
Chile[j]	Nationwide total	54.9	56.0	55.9	58.5	59.8	59.5	59.6	59.8	59.7	59.6	59.4
Colombia	Nationwide total	58.3	58.5	61.3	62.7	63.7	64.5	64.2	64.2	64.7	64.3	64.2
Costa Rica[h][k]	Nationwide total	57.0	56.7	60.4	59.1	60.7	62.5	62.2	62.6	61.2	61.7	57.8
Cuba[l]	Nationwide total	73.7	74.7	75.4	74.9	76.1	74.2	72.9	71.9	69.1	...	...
Dominican Republic	Nationwide total	64.3	63.7	61.4	62.6	63.8	64.7	64.2	64.8	64.9	64.4	65.0[g]
Ecuador	Nationwide total[l]	67.8	67.7	66.3	63.7	62.5	63.0	62.9	63.2	66.2	66.3	68.5
El Salvador	Nationwide total	62.1	62.7	62.8	62.5	62.7	63.2	63.6	62.8	62.1	...	...
Guatemala[m]	Nationwide total	60.1	...	...	54.3	61.8	65.4	60.6	60.9	60.7	60.4	61.5[n]
Honduras	Nationwide total	50.7	51.0	53.1	53.6	51.9	50.8	53.7	56.0	58.3	...	...
Jamaica	Nationwide total	64.9	65.4	63.5	62.4	62.3	61.9	63.0	62.8	63.1	63.0	64.8
Mexico	Nationwide total	58.8	58.7	58.6	58.4	58.6	59.2	60.3	59.8	59.8	59.6	59.7
Nicaragua[k]	Nationwide total	53.4	53.3	66.6	71.2	75.6	76.8	75.8	74.0	...	...	...
Panama	Nationwide total	62.7	63.9	64.1	63.5	61.9	63.4	64.1	64.0	64.2	64.2	64.4[o]
Paraguay	Nationwide total	60.8	61.7	62.9	60.5	60.7	64.3	62.6	61.6	61.6	...	...
Peru	Metropolitan Lima	68.9	68.1	68.4	70.0	70.0	69.1	68.9	68.4	68.3	68.0	68.3
Trinidad and Tobago	Nationwide total	63.5	63.5	62.7	62.1	61.3	61.8	61.3	61.9	60.6	60.8	60.1[p]
Uruguay	Nationwide total	62.5	62.7	63.4	62.9	64.8	64.0	63.6	64.7	63.8	63.6	63.4
Venezuela (Bolivarian Republic of)	Nationwide total	64.9	64.9	65.1	64.6	64.4	63.9	64.3	65.1	63.7	64.4	62.9[q]

Source: Economic Commission for Latin America and the Caribbean (ECLAC), on the basis of official figures.
[a] The figures in the last two columns refer to the period January-September.
[b] The regional series are weighted averages of national data (excluding the Belize and Nicaragua) and include adjustments for lack of information and changes in methodology. The data relating to the different countries are not comparable owing to differences in coverage and in the definition of the working-age population.
[c] The National Institute of Statistics and Censuses (INDEC) of Argentina does not recognize the data for the period 2007-2015 and has them under review. These data are therefore preliminary and will be replaced when new official data are published.
[d] The figures refer to the average from first to three quarters.
[e] The figures in the last two columns refer to the mesurement for May.
[f] The figures in the last two columns refer to the first quarter.
[g] The figures in the last two columns refer to the mesurement for April.
[h] New measurements have been used since 2012; the data are not comparable with the previous series.
[i] Up to 2011, the figures refer to six metropolitan areas.
[j] New measurements have been used since 2010; the data are not comparable with the previous series.
[k] New measurements have been used since 2009; the data are not comparable with the previous series.
[l] Up to 2009, urban areas.
[m] New measurements have been used since 2011; the data are not comparable with the previous series.
[n] The figures in the last two columns refer to the measurement for May 2015 and March 2016.
[o] The figures in the last two columns refer to the measurement for August.
[p] The figures in the last two columns refer to the measurement for March.
[q] The figures in the last two columns refer to the average January-April

Table A1.19
Latin America and the Caribbean: open urban unemployment[a]
(Average annual rates)

		2007	2008	2009	2010	2011	2012	2013	2014	2015	2016[b]
Latin America and the Caribbean[c]		**8.6**	**8.0**	**9.2**	**8.6**	**7.8**	**7.4**	**7.2**	**7.0**	**7.4**	**9.0**
Argentina[d]	Urban areas	8.5	7.9	8.7	7.7	7.2	7.2	7.1	7.3	6.5[e]	8.9[f]
Bahamas[g]	Nationwide total	7.9	8.7	14.2	...	15.9	14.4	15.8	14.8	13.4	12.7[h]
Guatemala[g]	Nationwide total	7.4	8.1	10.0	10.8	11.2	11.6	11.6	12.3	11.9	9.3[i]
Belize[g]	Nationwide total	8.5	8.2	13.1	12.5	...	15.3	13.2	11.6	10.1	8.0[j]
Bolivia (Plurinational State of)	Urban total	7.7	6.7	6.8	...	3.8	3.2	4.0	3.5	4.4	...
Brazil[k]	Twenty metropolitan areas[l]	9.3	7.9	8.1	6.7	6.0	8.2	8.0	7.8	9.3	12.9
Chile[m]	Nationwide total	7.1	7.8	9.7	8.2	7.1	6.4	5.9	6.4	6.2	6.5
Colombia[g]	Municipal capitals	12.2	12.1	13.2	12.7	11.8	11.4	10.7	10.0	9.8	10.3
Colombia[n]	Municipal capitals	11.2	11.4	12.4	12.0	11.1	10.8	10.0	9.4	9.2	9.7
Costa Rica[o]	Urban total	4.8	4.8	8.5	7.1	7.7	9.8	9.1	9.5	9.7	9.7[p]
Cuba	Nationwide total	1.8	1.6	1.7	2.5	3.2	3.5	3.3	2.7	2.4	...
Dominican Republic	Nationwide total	5.1	4.7	5.3	5.0	5.8	6.5	7.1	6.4	5.9	5.7[j]
Ecuador[g]	Urban total	7.4	6.9	8.5	7.6	6.0	4.9	4.7	5.1	5.4	6.7
Ecuador[n]	Urban total	5.5	5.4	6.9	6.1	5.0	4.2	4.0	4.3	4.7	6.0
El Salvador	Urban total	5.8	5.5	7.1	6.8	6.6	6.2	5.6	6.7	6.8	...
Guatemala[q]	Urban total	...	...	...	4.8	3.1	4.0	3.8	4.0	3.2	4.0[f]
Honduras	Urban total	4.0	4.1	4.9	6.4	6.8	5.6	6.0	7.5	8.8	...
Jamaica[g]	Nationwide total	9.8	10.6	11.4	12.4	12.6	13.9	15.2	13.7	13.5	13.3[p]
Jamaica[l]	Nationwide total	6.0	6.9	7.5	8.0	8.4	9.3	10.3	9.4	9.5	9.1[p]
Mexico	Urban total	4.0	4.3	5.9	5.9	5.6	5.4	5.4	5.3	4.7	4.3
Nicaragua	Urban total	7.3	8.0	10.5	10.1	6.5	7.6	...	...	...	...
Panama[g]	Urban total	7.8	6.5	7.9	7.7	5.4	4.8	4.7	5.4	5.8	6.4[s]
Panama[n]	Urban total	5.8	5.0	6.3	5.8	3.6	3.6	3.7	4.1	4.5	5.2[s]
Paraguay	Asuncion and urban areas of Central Department[t]	7.2	7.4	8.2	7.4	6.9	7.9	7.7	7.8	6.5	8.3[u]
Peru	Metropolitan Lima	8.4	8.4	8.4	7.9	7.7	6.8	5.9	5.9	6.5	6.7
Trinidad and Tobago[g]	Nationwide total	5.6	4.6	5.3	5.9	5.1	5.0	3.6	3.3	3.5	3.8[f]
Uruguay	Urban total	9.8	8.3	8.2	7.5	6.6	6.7	6.7	6.9	7.8	8.3
Venezuela (Bolivarian Republic of)[g]	Nationwide total	8.4	7.3	7.9	8.7	8.3	8.1	7.8	7.2	7.0	7.5[v]

Source: Economic Commission for Latin America and the Caribbean (ECLAC), on the basis of household surveys.

[a] Unemployed population as a percentage of the economically active population.

[b] Estimate based on data from January to September.

[c] Weighted average adjusted for lack of information and differences and changes in methodology. The data relating to the different countries are not comparable owing to differences in coverage and in the definition of the working age population.

[d] The National Institute of Statistics and Censuses (INDEC) of Argentina does not recognize the data for the period 2007-2015 and has them under review. These data are therefore preliminary and will be replaced when new official data are published.

[e] The figure refers to average from first to three quarters.

[f] The figure refer to the average for second and the three quarters.

[g] Includes hidden unemployment.

[h] Figures as of May.

[i] Figures as of first semester.

[j] Figures as of April.

[k] New measurements have been used since 2012; the data are not comparable with the previous series.

[l] Up to 2011, the figures refer to six metropolitan areas.

[m] New measurements have been used since 2010; the data are not comparable with the previous series.

[n] Includes an adjustment to the figures for the economically active population to exclude hidden unemployment.

[o] New measurements have been used since 2009; the data are not comparable with the previous series.

[p] January-September average.

[q] Owing to methodological changes, as of 2011 the data are not comparable with the previous series.

[r] Figures as of March.

[s] Figures as of August.

[t] Up to 2009, urban total.

[u] Figures as of first semester.

[v] January-April average.

Table A1.20

Latin America and the Caribbean: employment rate[a]

(Average annual rates)

		2007	2008	2009	2010	2011	2012	2013	2014	2015	2015	2016[b]
											January to September	
Latin America and the Caribbean[c]		**57.3**	**57.5**	**57.2**	**57.2**	**57.4**	**57.6**	**57.6**	**57.6**	**57.4**	...	...
Argentina[c]	Urban areas	54.5	54.2	54.2	54.4	55.2	55.0	54.7	54.0	53.9[d]	...	...
Bahamas	Nationwide total	70.2	69.7	63.0	...	60.6	64.1	61.6	62.8	64.3	64.2	67.1[e]
Barbados	Nationwide total	62.7	62.1	60.3	59.4	60.0	58.5	58.9	56.0	57.7	57.5	59.2[f]
Belize	Nationwide total	56.0	54.3	...	...	...	55.7	55.7	56.3	56.8	56.6	58.7[g]
Bolivia (Plurinational State of)	Nationwide total	61.4	63.1	63.0	...	64.1	59.8	61.6	64.4	...	...	...
Brazil[h]	Nationwide total[i]	51.6	52.5	52.1	53.2	53.7 |	56.9	56.9	56.8	56.1	56.1	54.4
Chile[j]	Nationwide total	51.0	51.7	50.5 |	53.7	55.5	55.7	56.0	56.0	56.0	55.8	55.5
Colombia[e]	Nationwide total	51.8	51.9	53.9	55.4	56.8	57.9	58.0	58.4	59.0	58.4	58.0
Costa Rica[h][k]	Nationwide total	54.4	53.9 |	55.4	54.8	56.0 |	56.2	56.4	56.6	55.4	55.7	52.3
Cuba[l]	Nationwide total	72.4	73.6	74.2	73.0	73.6	71.6	70.5	70.0	67.5	...	...
Dominican Republic	Nationwide total	54.2	54.7	52.3	53.6	54.5	55.2	54.6	55.4	55.8	55.4	56.4[g]
Ecuador	Nationwide total[m]	64.3	63.1	60.7 |	60.1	59.6	60.4	60.3	60.4	63.3	63.5	64.8
El Salvador	Nationwide total	58.1	59.0	59.2	58.1	58.6	59.4	59.9	58.4	57.8	...	...
Guatemala[l]	Nationwide total	58.6	...	...	... |	59.2	63.5	58.7	59.1	59.2	58.9	59.6[n]
Honduras	Nationwide total	49.2	49.4	51.5	51.5	49.7	48.9	51.6	53.1	54.0	...	...
Jamaica	Nationwide total	58.6	58.5	56.3 |	54.6	54.4	53.3	53.4	54.2	54.6	54.5	56.2
Mexico	Nationwide total	56.7	56.3	55.4	55.3	55.5	56.3	56.2	56.9	57.2	57.0	57.3
Nicaragua[k]	Nationwide total	48.6	50.1 |	61.3	65.6	71.2	72.3	71.5	69.1	...	...	...
Panama	Nationwide total	58.7	60.3	59.9	59.4	59.1	60.8	61.5	60.9	60.9	60.9	60.8[o]
Paraguay	Nationwide total	57.4	57.0	57.1	57.1	57.3	61.2	59.4	57.9	58.3	...	...
Peru	Metropolitan Lima	63.0	62.4	62.7	64.5	64.5	64.4	64.8	64.3	63.8	63.4	63.6
Trinidad and Tobago	Nationwide total	59.9	60.6	59.4	58.4	58.2	58.8	59.1	59.9	58.9	58.6	57.8[p]
Uruguay	Nationwide total	56.7	57.7	58.5	58.4	60.7	59.9	59.5	60.4	59.0	58.9	58.4
Venezuela (Bolivarian Republic of)	Nationwide total	59.5	60.2	60.0	59.0	59.0	58.7	59.3	60.4	59.2	59.8	58.2[q]

Source: Economic Commission for Latin America and the Caribbean (ECLAC), on the basis of official figures.

[a] Employed population as a percentage of the working-age population.

[b] The regional series are weighted averages of national data (excluding Belize and Nicaragua) and include adjustement for lack of information and changes in methology. These data are therefore preliminary and will be replaced when new official data are published. The data relating to the different countries are not comparable owing to differences in coverage and in the definition of the working age population.

[c] The National Institute of Statistics and Censuses (INDEC) of Argentina does not recognize the data for the period 2007-2015 and has them under review. These data are therefore preliminary and will be replaced when new official data are published.

[d] The figure refers to average from first to three quarters.

[e] The figures in the last two columns correspond to the mesurement for May.

[f] The figure in the last two columns refer to the first quarter

[g] The figures in the last two columns correspond to the mesurement for April.

[h] New measurements have been used since 2012; the data are not comparable with the previous series.

[i] Up to 2011, the figures refer to six metropolitan areas.

[j] New measurements have been used since 2010; the data are not comparable with the previous series.

[k] New measurements have been used since 2009; the data are not comparable with the previous series.

[l] Owing to methodological changes, as of 2011 the data are not comparable with the previous series.

[m] Up to 2009, urban total.

[n] The figures in the last two columns refer to the measurement for May 2015 and March 2016.

[o] The figures in the last two columns correspond to the mesurement for August.

[p] The figures in the last two columns correspond to the mesurement for March.

[q] The figures in the last two columns correspond to the January-April average.

Table A1.21
Latin America: real average wages[a]
(Index 2010=100)

	2007	2008	2009	2010	2011	2012	2013	2014	2015	2016[b]
Bolivia (Plurinational State of)[c]	102.2	94.4	96.5	100.0	98.2	99.3	100.3	101.8	108.6	...
Brazil[d]	94.3	96.3	98.5	100.0	101.4	104.9	107.1	108.8	105.3	103.8
Chile[e]	93.6	93.4	97.9	100.0	102.5	105.8	109.9	111.9	113.9	115.4
Colombia[f]	97.6	96.1	97.3	100.0	100.3	101.3	104.0	104.5	105.4	103.8
Costa Rica[g]	92.8	90.9	97.9	100.0	105.7	107.1	108.5	110.7	115.2	119.7
Cuba	95.8	95.3	99.7	100.0	100.2	100.7	101.2	124.0	143.1	...
El Salvador[h]	98.7	95.6	98.9	100.0	97.1	97.3	97.8	98.5	106.3	...
Guatemala[g]	99.7	97.1	97.2	100.0	100.4	104.4	104.3	106.8	110.4	...
Mexico[g]	101.7	101.9	100.9	100.0	100.8	101.0	100.9	101.3	102.8	103.8
Nicaragua[g]	97.2	93.3	98.8	100.0	100.1	100.5	100.7	102.4	105.2	106.4
Panama	94.7	90.9	93.3	100.0	100.1	103.5	103.8	109.5	113.1	118.0[i]
Paraguay	95.7	95.0	99.4	100.0	102.8	103.5	105.7	107.0	107.5	...
Peru[j]	97.9	100.0	103.1	100.0	108.4	111.0	114.7	117.9	117.5	119.5
Uruguay	87.1	90.2	96.8	100.0	104.0	108.4	111.7	115.4	117.3	118.9
Venezuela (Bolivarian Republic of)	117.4	112.1	105.6	100.0	103.0	109.1	104.3	...	...	...

Source: Economic Commission for Latin America and the Caribbean (ECLAC), on the basis of official figures.

[a] Figures deflated by the official consumer price index of each country.
[b] Estimate based on data from January to September.
[c] Private-sector average wage index.
[d] Private-sector workers covered by social and labour legislation.
[e] General index of hourly remuneration.
[f] Manufacturing.
[g] Average wage declared by workers registered with and paying into social security.
[h] Average taxable wage.
[i] Estimate based on interannual grwoth of average for January-June.
[j] Payroll workers in the Lima metropolitan area. Until 2010, formal private sector workers in the Lima metropolitan area.

Table A1.22
Latin America and the Caribbean: monetary indicators
(Percentage variation with respect to the year-earlier period)

		2007	2008	2009	2010	2011	2012	2013	2014	2015	2016[a]
Latin America											
Argentina	Monetary base	29.0	19.1	5.4	25.1	37.1	34.9	30.2	19.7	33.2	28.0
	Money (M1)	23.4	16.7	13.0	24.1	32.4	33.3	29.5	26.1	31.6	22.2[b]
	M2	24.5	18.1	5.9	27.6	36.9	32.4	30.9	23.1	33.2	25.3[b]
	Foreign-currency deposits	27.8	36.4	61.6	35.9	8.7	-22.6	-6.1	51.7	38.5	141.8[b]
Bolivia (Plurinational State of)	Monetary base	48.2	53.8	19.6	32.4	11.6	18.2	10.8	9.5	19.2	9.7[c]
	Money (M1)	55.2	50.2	9.4	24.1	27.2	18.3	13.5	15.4	9.4	10.6[c]
	M2	68.1	59.6	18.4	34.6	34.0	31.3	22.6	18.8	18.4	15.3[c]
	Foreign-currency deposits	11.2	-9.2	20.4	4.7	-12.8	-5.0	-4.1	-3.4	3.7	0.4[c]
Brazil	Monetary base	20.9	12.5	8.0	17.5	11.0	9.4	5.5	7.2	3.0	3.1
	Money (M1)	23.3	11.8	7.4	17.5	6.1	5.9	10.7	4.7	-1.6	-1.7
	M2	14.1	30.3	22.1	11.1	21.0	13.4	9.3	11.7	6.8	5.2
Chile	Monetary base	20.8	7.0	15.0	13.8	14.8	13.7	16.3	5.3	9.6	10.1
	Money (M1)	17.9	11.1	14.1	27.7	10.9	9.1	10.1	12.1	14.3	7.9
	M2	20.3	17.7	3.7	5.1	14.7	14.7	9.7	8.7	11.1	10.5
	Foreign-currency deposits	11.6	40.7	2.6	8.5	11.8	8.9	18.7	29.0	18.7	8.6
Colombia	Monetary base	18.1	14.3	10.3	12.4	15.1	9.5	12.5	16.7	15.0	12.4
	Money (M1)	13.5	8.0	9.7	14.7	16.2	6.7	14.3	14.8	10.4	5.5
	M2	18.7	14.6	13.2	6.9	14.8	16.9	17.5	12.9	10.1	11.6
Costa Rica	Monetary base	25.4	25.7	6.3	10.0	11.7	12.1	14.1	11.7	11.1	10.9
	Money (M1)	41.1	21.7	-3.4	9.5	19.2	9.4	11.9	13.0	9.3	20.4
	M2	34.9	22.9	1.3	2.6	11.1	13.8	13.0	14.4	9.4	4.2
	Foreign-currency deposits	7.2	10.7	36.8	-1.9	-7.1	-1.2	0.1	13.0	1.8	2.0
Dominican Republic	Monetary base	18.4	12.3	3.4	6.4	5.8	9.0	3.9	3.3	22.1	9.5
	Money (M1)	26.6	11.0	-1.1	17.5	4.9	7.3	12.1	13.6	12.9	14.2
	M2	14.2	10.9	7.6	13.5	8.8	12.1	8.0	11.2	10.7	12.6
	Foreign-currency deposits	10.7	15.0	4.4	18.9	17.8	18.4	16.1	11.5	11.9	9.6
Ecuador	Monetary base	...	16.4	18.1	24.1	9.9	16.1	23.3	17.5	10.1	21.9[b]
	Money (M1)	...	44.5	38.0	16.1	15.5	14.0	14.8	14.4	10.6	8.2[b]
	M2	...	33.0	22.0	18.6	20.0	17.8	13.4	14.5	6.7	3.3[b]
El Salvador	Monetary base	13.9	8.1	10.8	0.4	-1.3	1.8	4.8	2.8	1.2	3.1
	Money (M1)	12.2	8.5	7.6	19.8	10.4	4.4	2.9	4.0	4.9	5.9[b]
	M2	15.0	6.1	0.9	1.6	-2.1	0.5	1.8	0.8	3.7	6.1[b]
Guatemala	Monetary base	17.3	4.1	6.6	8.0	10.1	5.8	9.2	5.8	12.1	9.0
	Money (M1)	17.6	3.4	7.6	7.2	9.1	5.8	7.0	5.2	11.9	6.0
	M2	11.7	7.3	9.4	8.4	10.6	9.4	9.7	8.1	11.5	8.0
	Foreign-currency deposits	4.2	9.9	18.1	11.6	4.9	3.2	11.2	9.4	6.0	4.3
Haiti	Monetary base	11.3	16.1	14.2	34.1	18.1	9.2	0.4	-1.0	15.4	29.8[d]
	Money (M1)	3.5	21.4	9.2	26.9	14.4	8.7	11.1	8.7	12.7	2.3[d]
	M2	5.3	13.7	6.9	17.4	11.5	5.7	9.4	8.4	11.9	8.1[d]
	Foreign-currency deposits	3.2	22.1	14.4	22.5	18.4	6.9	8.2	8.5	18.5	31.9[d]
Honduras	Monetary base	31.3	24.8	11.6	-13.8	10.7	11.3	4.0	9.7	16.6	12.4[b]
	Money (M1)	18.4	11.5	2.2	5.2	17.7	2.1	-5.0	8.4	19.0	9.8[b]
	M2	19.4	9.2	0.8	4.7	17.2	8.7	3.6	8.9	12.8	10.0[b]
	Foreign-currency deposits	10.5	20.3	-1.0	5.4	7.8	15.3	12.6	7.3	11.2	5.7[b]

Table A1.22 (continued)

		2007	2008	2009	2010	2011	2012	2013	2014	2015	2016[a]
Mexico	Monetary base	12.6	12.6	15.9	9.7	9.5	13.9	6.3	13.5	20.1	16.0
	Money (M1)	11.6	8.5	11.8	11.2	16.2	13.7	7.5	13.9	16.1	11.8
	M2	7.5	13.9	11.5	5.8	12.4	10.7	7.1	11.0	13.5	9.8
	Foreign-currency deposits	-6.4	2.8	20.7	0.9	3.0	16.8	13.3	26.6	40.0	26.3
Nicaragua	Monetary base	18.3	15.2	0.7	24.0	20.5	18.3	6.3	12.9	17.4	13.0
	Money (M1)	18.2	32.9	4.4	21.4	24.8	17.6	8.5	16.5	21.0	10.3[b]
	M2	18.2	32.9	4.4	21.4	24.8	17.6	8.5	16.5	21.0	10.3[b]
	Foreign-currency deposits	8.0	10.2	5.3	25.8	7.8	21.2	13.6	20.4	16.3	15.8[b]
Panama	Monetary base	9.6	17.7	11.2	7.5	27.1	12.7	16.0	-1.2	28.5	11.0[b]
	Money (M1)	29.2	26.5	17.4	19.2	21.5	17.1	6.9	13.6	0.9	0.1[b]
	M2	22.4	17.1	9.2	11.3	9.9	10.8	6.3	12.4	5.6	6.1[b]
Paraguay	Monetary base	31.2	27.6	30.7	5.2	5.0	11.8	5.1	8.3	11.3	1.9
	Money (M1)	34.4	30.5	6.6	28.7	7.8	8.6	15.6	9.6	11.6	1.5
	M2	34.2	38.4	13.3	26.4	14.0	13.7	17.4	10.6	11.2	2.7
	Depósitos en moneda extranjera	9.3	21.1	40.1	16.4	13.5	14.9	15.8	29.3	22.3	17.7
Peru	Monetary base	25.2	38.2	2.1	24.2	31.3	31.2	21.1	-8.6	-0.9	1.9[b]
	Money (M1)	30.6	31.3	8.8	28.0	19.7	18.7	14.3	4.9	5.1	4.4
	M2	37.7	48.5	-2.2	27.8	18.7	23.2	18.4	2.5	2.9	9.0
	Foreign-currency deposits	7.9	11.2	23.1	-0.1	13.8	0.4	16.3	21.4	17.3	11.8
Uruguay	Monetary base	28.9	28.6	6.1	12.9	23.1	21.8	15.3	11.0	11.5	13.2
	Money (M1)	23.0	22.4	13.1	24.6	19.6	18.4	11.7	6.1	7.1	1.1
	M2	22.5	26.1	11.3	25.8	26.0	17.4	12.4	8.7	9.4	10.3
	Foreign-currency deposits	2.2	3.1	24.1	2.3	10.7	19.6	14.8	25.8	26.6	23.5
Venezuela (Bolivarian Republic of)	Monetary base	65.5	39.5	18.3	24.5	27.0	40.8	61.1	86.5	95.2	110.9
	Money (M1)	66.8	24.3	28.8	27.5	44.8	62.0	66.1	69.5	85.1	100.5[b]
	M2	60.2	16.9	28.3	18.0	37.6	57.5	65.4	69.1	84.9	100.9[b]
The Caribbean											
Antigua and Barbuda	Monetary base	10.0	2.0	-10.5	0.9	20.1	29.4	13.2	20.0	14.4	13.2[b]
	Money (M1)	16.4	6.7	-14.2	-7.3	-6.6	-2.1	3.1	11.5	4.4	11.8[b]
	M2	11.3	7.6	-2.9	-3.1	-1.1	1.7	2.8	3.5	2.5	-0.5[b]
	Foreign-currency deposits	32.0	-0.5	39.9	-45.2	5.8	-12.8	0.9	20.0	17.0	25.7[b]
Bahamas	Monetary base	17.2	6.4	2.0	2.5	26.8	-7.8	2.2	13.8	-1.8	15.0[d]
	Money (M1)	1.5	0.3	-0.2	2.8	6.2	8.6	5.6	8.4	18.7	3.8[d]
	M2	8.5	6.5	2.8	2.8	2.3	1.1	-0.6	0.1	1.5	1.3[d]
	Foreign-currency deposits	17.7	15.9	8.4	0.1	-2.7	11.6	15.8	-1.5	-19.9	-12.8[d]
Barbados	Monetary base	26.8	9.2	-13.9	3.4	7.7	-0.9	10.6	5.8	31.5	22.1[c]
	Money (M1)	11.9	7.7	-5.3	1.7	-0.5	-20.3	5.5	9.4	14.1	18.2[d]
	M2	11.7	9.3	-1.0	-0.8	0.3	-5.7	3.5	1.5	3.4	5.2[d]
Belize	Monetary base	15.1	11.5	11.9	-1.2	8.2	17.5	19.2	18.8	24.6	18.4[b]
	Money (M1)	17.0	9.2	-1.9	-0.9	9.1	24.0	13.7	14.0	14.6	15.1[c]
Dominica	Monetary base	6.5	-0.1	-4.6	9.7	8.5	17.8	-0.0	15.0	19.1	27.3[b]
	Money (M1)	10.1	4.4	-1.3	-1.5	-2.1	9.8	2.5	2.2	7.8	17.5[b]
	M2	10.5	8.2	7.5	3.8	3.2	7.0	4.5	6.5	4.3	6.0[b]
	Foreign-currency deposits	-0.6	19.0	15.9	30.2	38.8	25.4	-6.1	13.5	1.3	-8.9[b]
Grenada	Monetary base	9.2	3.5	-8.5	6.0	7.2	4.7	5.4	21.1	6.1	5.0[b]
	Money (M1)	7.1	3.1	-12.9	3.8	-7.3	2.9	5.4	24.1	20.6	12.8[b]
	M2	5.2	8.1	1.0	3.4	0.4	1.8	3.0	5.2	3.7	2.0[b]
	Foreign-currency deposits	26.0	2.7	17.4	-3.9	-5.5	5.5	-18.8	7.8	17.4	45.7[b]
Guyana	Monetary base	0.8	16.5	10.6	17.7	17.4	15.2	6.6	2.5	14.3	13.4[b]
	Money (M1)	20.5	18.6	8.2	12.9	21.9	16.1	6.7	10.1	7.9	5.5[b]

Table A1.22 (concluded)

		2007	2008	2009	2010	2011	2012	2013	2014	2015	2016[a]
Jamaica	Monetary base	15.1	9.5	22.8	5.5	5.3	6.3	6.3	5.9	9.9	15.7
	Money (M1)	18.8	9.1	7.6	7.0	7.8	4.7	5.9	5.0	15.7	18.0[c]
	M2	14.3	7.9	4.4	6.1	5.6	3.3	6.4	2.6	9.9	13.1[c]
	Foreign-currency deposits	18.2	10.9	17.5	-0.9	-4.8	6.8	28.5	9.2	15.6	21.5[c]
Saint Kitts and Nevis	Monetary base	15.7	7.3	48.3	-3.2	36.1	13.7	22.2	10.5	-14.5	16.7[b]
	Money (M1)	17.4	7.2	9.2	16.8	28.6	18.2	12.3	1.6	10.8	2.3[b]
	M2	11.9	10.3	10.2	9.4	10.7	8.8	6.4	6.4	5.9	1.9[b]
	Foreign-currency deposits	16.4	-9.2	-7.0	-9.0	-1.0	6.4	35.6	46.4	16.3	-6.5[b]
Saint Lucia	Monetary base	14.4	10.2	8.5	3.6	16.3	4.2	8.0	8.0	25.2	4.8[b]
	Money (M1)	5.0	7.1	-2.4	-4.3	4.0	3.2	2.2	7.1	3.0	3.6[b]
	M2	11.3	10.7	4.1	0.2	4.9	3.7	3.5	-1.0	1.6	2.6[b]
	Foreign-currency deposits	47.8	8.9	9.3	-13.2	16.4	14.0	-10.1	45.0	20.1	18.6[b]
Saint Vincent and the Grenadines	Monetary base	4.5	2.0	-3.2	11.9	0.8	11.8	26.2	16.9	8.3	17.2[b]
	Money (M1)	6.8	-1.4	-8.3	-0.5	-3.9	-0.4	9.6	5.8	8.6	8.6[b]
	M2	9.5	1.9	0.8	2.2	1.9	1.2	8.6	8.1	5.6	4.4[b]
	Foreign-currency deposits	102.1	1.5	-6.5	-7.7	30.8	-7.3	29.2	15.6	17.6	13.2[b]
Suriname	Monetary base	39.7	30.2	22.1	13.0	3.2	27.0	13.8	-7.2	-6.2	34.3
	Money (M1)	26.7	21.3	26.3	16.7	5.3	17.0	11.3	5.4	-5.1	16.1[b]
	M2	30.2	21.0	25.1	18.2	7.0	20.0	17.7	8.1	-2.8	11.5[b]
	Foreign-currency deposits	25.7	24.3	12.0	7.9	39.1	13.6	10.8	11.4	9.9	77.3[b]
Trinidad and Tobago	Monetary base	19.0	32.3	37.6	24.7	14.1	15.4	19.5	8.0	-7.9	-7.7[c]
	Money (M1)	7.6	17.6	24.0	25.5	17.2	15.4	19.2	19.8	0.0	0.8[c]
	M2	13.3	17.2	17.6	17.9	8.4	12.0	11.8	11.6	3.8	3.0[c]
	Foreign-currency deposits	36.4	21.1	32.2	7.9	-4.0	4.7	12.6	-5.6	0.8	...

Source: Economic Commission for Latin America and the Caribbean (ECLAC), on the basis of official figures.
[a] Figures as of September.
[b] Figures as of August.
[c] Figures as of July.
[d] Figures as of June.

Table A1.23

Latin America and the Caribbean: domestic credit

(Percentage variation with respect to the year-earlier period)

	2007	2008	2009	2010	2011	2012	2013	2014	2015	2016[a]
Latin America										
Argentina	1.7	23.9	2.3	51.3	59.5	33.0	40.8	24.7	36.2	27.8[b]
Bolivia (Plurinational State of)	6.5	7.5	10.9	13.0	18.8	22.7	21.6	17.6	16.7	18.8[c]
Brazil	20.1	15.8	11.3	18.0	17.6	16.8	11.9	9.5	9.0	9.8[b]
Chile	15.6	18.4	6.6	-0.1	12.1	15.1	9.3	7.6	8.4	9.9[d]
Colombia	15.4	15.7	14.4	25.9	19.0	15.7	13.8	12.2	16.6	9.7[e]
Costa Rica	22.1	21.1	19.1	4.6	12.4	11.7	9.2	19.9	15.5	13.6
Dominican Republic	10.7	17.4	12.3	7.5	9.5	12.1	12.4	11.6	14.9	15.4
Ecuador	18.2	1.7	20.8	33.6	31.5	21.5	16.7	16.2	10.1	2.2[b]
El Salvador	12.4	11.3	2.4	2.2	3.5	9.6	5.5	9.5	7.3	8.7
Guatemala	13.8	10.4	5.2	5.6	15.2	11.3	12.6	12.0	12.0	6.8
Haiti	0.3	7.8	9.7	-23.0	-17.1	11.4	70.0	30.4	18.2	10.7[e]
Honduras	49.0	27.1	6.7	10.0	10.8	18.0	9.6	6.8	7.9	5.0
Mexico	21.6	8.7	16.7	10.6	11.3	10.7	9.4	9.8	12.3	13.7[e]
Nicaragua	11.4	16.7	-1.2	-4.6	-6.2	21.6	21.4	11.3	13.4	13.4
Panama	10.7	15.9	1.2	9.5	18.8	18.1	12.9	15.4	6.4	10.5
Paraguay	11.0	33.5	12.7	36.3	25.5	28.4	20.8	12.0	26.0	9.4
Peru	38.0	9.4	9.9	24.1	12.0	9.6	6.6	18.6	14.2	12.5
Uruguay	...	...	...	3.9	24.7	19.4	16.5	18.6	12.9	41.1[b]
Venezuela (Bolivarian Republic of)[f]	51.6	22.0	28.4	13.7	36.0	56.1	61.9	63.8	74.5	92.0[b]
The Caribbean										
Antigua and Barbuda	17.3	12.5	19.9	0.6	-3.8	-3.0	-4.9	-0.4	-5.9	-13.9[b]
Bahamas	4.8	7.5	5.3	3.4	0.8	4.0	1.9	-0.0	0.7	0.8[e]
Barbados	8.2	10.1	6.4	-0.5	-0.9	6.6	8.0	2.3	3.2	9.2[g]
Belize	13.7	8.9	5.7	-0.4	-1.6	0.4	-2.6	-0.6	8.9	22.2[b]
Dominica	-9.3	5.0	8.5	12.5	13.7	7.6	7.7	1.7	-1.8	-20.7[b]
Grenada	15.4	13.1	8.9	3.9	2.6	5.0	-2.1	-9.0	-10.2	-11.9[b]
Guyana	28.9	15.8	4.5	-0.8	34.5	40.1	26.3	16.0	11.3	13.8[b]
Jamaica	12.4	16.3	15.0	-3.4	-4.1	11.7	16.0	14.2	-2.2	1.7[d]
Saint Kitts and Nevis	9.9	3.0	6.2	6.3	0.2	-9.0	-20.9	-18.7	-2.3	-3.5[b]
Saint Lucia	29.6	21.1	4.6	-0.3	2.9	6.6	5.4	-3.1	-12.2	-6.2[b]
Saint Vincent and the Grenadines	16.5	9.5	7.1	1.5	-7.2	-1.0	6.4	3.5	5.4	1.3[b]
Suriname	20.7	18.5	16.9	21.4	20.8	10.3	23.5	21.5	23.5	43.1[b]
Trinidad and Tobago	90.1	6.5	35.5	36.6	9.3	7.9	-20.4	-23.8	3.2	35.1[b]

Source: Economic Commission for Latin America and the Caribbean (ECLAC), on the basis of official figures.

[a] Figures as of September.

[b] Figures as of August.

[c] Figures as of March.

[d] Figures as of July.

[e] Figures as of June.

[f] Credit granted by the commercial and universal banks.

[g] Figures as of May.

Table A1.24
Latin America and the Caribbean: monetary policy rates
(Average rates)

	2007	2008	2009	2010	2011	2012	2013	2014	2015	2016[a]
Latin America										
Argentina	9.1	11.3	14.0	12.3	11.8	12.8	14.6	26.7	27.0	29.7[b]
Bolivia (Plurinational State of)	6.0	9.0	7.0	3.0	4.0	4.0	4.1	5.1	2.7	2.5[b]
Brazil	12.0	12.4	10.1	9.9	11.8	8.5	8.4	11.0	13.6	14.2
Chile	5.3	7.2	1.8	1.5	4.8	5.0	4.9	3.7	3.1	3.5
Colombia	8.8	9.8	5.8	3.2	4.0	4.9	3.4	3.9	4.7	7.0
Costa Rica	6.0	8.0	9.6	8.1	5.6	5.0	4.4	4.9	3.5	1.8
Dominican Republic	7.3	9.0	5.1	4.2	6.4	5.8	5.3	6.3	5.4	5.1
Guatemala	5.5	6.9	5.5	4.5	4.9	5.2	5.1	4.6	3.3	3.0[b]
Haiti	11.6	6.9	6.2	5.0	3.2	3.0	3.0	4.8	12.3	15.0[b]
Honduras	6.3	8.4	4.9	4.5	4.8	6.6	7.0	7.0	6.5	5.8[b]
Mexico	7.2	7.9	5.4	4.5	4.5	4.5	3.9	3.2	3.0	4.1
Paraguay	6.0	5.9	2.1	2.2	7.9	6.0	5.5	6.7	6.1	5.8
Peru	4.7	5.9	3.3	2.1	4.0	4.3	4.2	3.8	3.4	4.2
Uruguay[c]	...	7.4	8.5	6.3	7.5	8.8	9.3	...	...	...
Venezuela (Bolivarian Republic of)	9.8	12.3	8.1	6.3	6.4	6.4	6.2	6.4	6.2	6.5[d]
The Caribbean										
Antigua and Barbuda	6.5	6.5	6.5	6.5	6.5	6.5	6.5	6.5	6.5	6.5[b]
Bahamas	5.3	5.3	5.3	5.3	4.8	4.5	4.5	4.5	4.5	4.5[b]
Barbados	12.0	11.8	7.9	7.0	7.0	7.0	7.0	7.0	7.0	7.0[b]
Belize	18.0	18.0	18.0	18.0	11.0	11.0	11.0	11.0	11.0	11.0[b]
Dominica	6.5	6.5	6.5	6.5	6.5	6.5	6.5	6.5	6.5	6.5[b]
Grenada	6.5	6.5	6.5	6.5	6.5	6.5	6.5	6.5	6.5	6.5[b]
Guyana	6.5	6.6	6.9	6.4	5.4	5.4	5.0	5.0	5.0	5.0[b]
Jamaica	11.7	14.1	14.8	9.0	6.6	6.3	5.8	5.8	5.5	5.2[d]
Saint Kitts and Nevis	6.5	6.5	6.5	6.5	6.5	6.5	6.5	6.5	6.5	6.5[b]
Saint Lucia	6.5	6.5	6.5	6.5	6.5	6.5	6.5	6.5	6.5	6.5[b]
Saint Vincent and the Grenadines	6.5	6.5	6.5	6.5	6.5	6.5	6.5	6.5	6.5	6.5[b]
Trinidad and Tobago	8.0	8.4	7.5	4.7	3.2	2.9	2.8	2.8	4.1	4.8

Source: Economic Commission for Latin America and the Caribbean (ECLAC), on the basis of official figures.
[a] Figures as of November.
[b] Figures as of October.
[c] As of June 2013, the interest rate was no longer used as an instrument of monetary policy.
[d] Figures as of August.

Table A1.25
Latin America and the Caribbean: representative lending rates
(Average rates)

	2007	2008	2009	2010	2011	2012	2013	2014	2015	2016[a]
Latin America										
Argentina[b]	14.0	19.8	21.3	15.2	17.7	19.3	21.6	29.3	28.2	34.4
Bolivia (Plurinational State of)[c]	8.3	8.9	8.5	5.2	6.3	6.7	7.0	6.5	6.4	6.2
Brazil[d]	51.0	54.1	47.5	42.9	44.7	39.6	38.8	44.6	49.1	53.1
Chile[e]	13.6	15.2	12.9	11.8	12.4	13.5	13.2	10.8	9.3	10.3
Colombia[f]	17.9	19.6	15.6	12.4	12.8	13.7	12.2	12.1	12.1	14.7
Costa Rica[g]	17.3	16.7	21.6	19.8	18.1	19.7	17.4	16.6	15.9	14.7
Dominican Republic[h]	...	...	...	...	...	15.5	13.6	13.9	14.9	15.1
Ecuador[i]	10.1	9.8	9.2	9.0	8.3	8.2	8.2	8.1	8.3	8.8
El Salvador[j]	7.8	7.9	9.3	7.6	6.0	5.6	5.7	6.0	6.2	6.3
Guatemala[g]	12.8	13.4	13.8	13.3	13.4	13.5	13.6	13.8	13.2	13.1
Haiti[k]	31.2	23.3	21.6	20.7	19.8	19.4	18.9	18.6	18.8	19.8
Honduras[g]	16.6	17.9	19.4	18.9	18.6	18.4	20.1	20.6	20.7	19.5[l]
Mexico[m]	...	...	...	...	29.9	28.6	27.9	28.6	28.5	26.4[n]
Nicaragua[o]	13.0	13.2	14.0	13.3	10.8	12.0	15.0	13.5	12.0	11.5
Panama[p]	8.3	8.2	8.3	7.9	7.3	7.0	7.4	7.6	7.6	7.6[l]
Paraguay[q]	12.8	13.5	14.6	12.5	16.9	16.6	16.6	15.7	14.4	15.9[l]
Peru[r]	22.9	23.7	21.0	19.0	18.7	19.2	18.1	15.7	16.1	16.3
Uruguay[s]	10.0	13.1	16.6	12.0	11.0	12.0	13.3	17.2	17.0	17.8
Venezuela (Bolivarian Republic of)[t]	16.7	22.8	20.6	18.0	17.4	16.2	15.6	17.2	20.0	21.3
The Caribbean										
Antigua and Barbuda[h]	10.3	10.1	9.5	10.2	10.1	9.4	9.4	9.6	8.7	9.2[l]
Bahamas[u]	10.6	11.0	10.6	11.0	11.0	10.9	11.2	11.8	12.3	12.4[l]
Barbados[h]	9.6	9.3	8.8	8.3	8.1	7.2	7.0	7.0	6.9	6.7[l]
Belize[v]	14.3	14.1	14.1	13.9	13.3	12.3	11.5	10.9	10.3	9.9[l]
Dominica[h]	9.2	9.4	10.0	9.4	8.7	8.9	9.0	8.8	8.6	8.3[l]
Grenada[h]	9.7	9.4	10.7	10.3	10.4	9.5	9.1	9.1	8.8	8.5[l]
Guyana[h]	14.1	13.9	14.0	15.2	14.7	14.0	12.1	11.1	10.8	10.8[l]
Jamaica[h]	21.6	21.4	21.5	20.4	20.0	18.6	17.7	17.2	17.0	16.6[l]
Saint Kitts and Nevis[h]	9.3	8.6	8.6	8.5	9.2	8.5	8.4	8.8	8.5	8.4[l]
Saint Lucia[h]	9.7	9.3	9.5	9.5	9.2	8.6	8.4	8.4	8.5	8.2[l]
Saint Vincent and the Grenadines[h]	9.6	9.5	9.1	9.0	9.0	9.3	9.2	9.3	9.3	9.1[l]
Suriname[w]	13.8	12.0	11.7	11.7	11.8	11.7	12.0	12.3	12.6	13.3[l]
Trinidad and Tobago[h]	11.8	12.4	12.0	9.5	8.2	8.0	7.8	7.7	8.3	9.1

Source: Economic Commission for Latin America and the Caribbean (ECLAC), on the basis of official figures.
[a] Figures as of October.
[b] Local-currency loans to the non-financial private sector, at fixed or renegotiable rates, signature loans of up to 89 days.
[c] Nominal local-currency rate for 60-91-day operations.
[d] Interest rate on total consumer credit.
[e] Non-adjustable 90-360 day operations.
[f] Weighted average of consumer, prime, ordinary and treasury lending rates for the working days of the month.
[g] Weighted average of the system lending rates in local currency.
[h] Business credit, 30-367 days.
[i] Effective benchmark lending rate for the corporate commercial segment.
[j] Basic lending rate for up to one year.
[k] Average of minimum and maximum lending rates.
[l] Figures as of September.
[m] Average interest rate for credit cards from commercial banks and average interest rate for mortgage loans.
[n] Figures as of August.
[o] Weighted average of short-term lending rates in local currency.
[p] Interest rate on one-year trade credit.
[q] Commercial lending rate, local currency.
[r] Market lending rate, average for transactions conducted in the last 30 business days.
[s] Average rate for loan operations for the six major commercial banks.
[t] Weighted average of lending rates.
[u] Weighted average of lending and overdraft rates.
[v] Rate for personal and business loans, residential and other construction loans; weighted average.
[w] Average of lending rates.

Table A1.26
Latin America and the Caribbean: consumer prices
(12-month percentage variation)

	2007	2008	2009	2010	2011	2012	2013	2014	2015	2016[a]
Latin America and the Caribbean[b]	**6.3**	**8.3**	**4.6**	**6.5**	**6.8**	**5.7**	**7.5**	**9.4**	**16.5**	**...**
Latin America and the Caribbean[c]	**5.6**	**7.0**	**3.5**	**5.4**	**5.8**	**4.9**	**5.0**	**6.3**	**7.9**	**8.4**
Latin America										
Argentina	8.5	7.2	7.7	10.9	9.5	10.8	10.9	23.9	27.5	42.4
Bolivia (Plurinational State of)	11.7	11.9	0.3	7.2	6.9	4.5	6.5	5.2	3.0	3.5
Brazil	4.5	5.9	4.3	5.9	6.5	5.8	5.9	6.4	10.7	8.5
Chile	7.8	7.1	-1.4	3.0	4.4	1.5	3.0	4.6	4.4	3.1
Colombia	5.7	7.7	2.0	3.2	3.7	2.4	1.9	3.7	6.8	7.3
Costa Rica	10.8	13.9	4.0	5.8	4.7	4.5	3.7	5.1	-0.8	0.4
Cuba[d]	10.6	-0.1	-0.1	1.5	1.3	2.0	0.0	2.1	2.8	-0.8
Dominican Republic	8.9	4.5	5.7	6.3	7.8	3.9	3.9	1.6	2.3	1.4
Ecuador	3.3	8.8	4.3	3.3	5.4	4.2	2.7	3.7	3.4	1.3
El Salvador	4.9	5.5	-0.2	2.1	5.1	0.8	0.8	0.5	1.0	1.0
Guatemala	8.7	9.4	-0.3	5.4	6.2	3.4	4.4	2.9	3.1	4.6
Haiti	9.9	10.1	2.0	6.2	8.3	7.6	3.4	6.4	12.5	12.5
Honduras	8.9	10.8	3.0	6.5	5.6	5.4	4.9	5.8	2.4	2.9
Mexico	3.8	6.5	3.6	4.4	3.8	3.6	4.0	4.1	2.1	3.0
Nicaragua	16.2	12.7	1.8	9.1	8.6	7.1	5.4	6.4	2.9	3.5
Panama	6.4	6.8	1.9	4.9	6.3	4.6	3.7	1.0	0.3	1.2
Paraguay	6.0	7.5	1.9	7.2	4.9	4.0	3.7	4.2	3.1	3.5
Peru	3.9	6.7	0.2	2.1	4.7	2.6	2.9	3.2	4.4	3.1
Uruguay	8.5	9.2	5.9	6.9	8.6	7.5	8.5	8.3	9.4	8.9
Venezuela (Bolivarian Republic of)[e]	22.5	31.9	25.1	27.2	27.6	20.1	56.2	68.5	180.9	...
The Caribbean										
Antigua and Barbuda	5.2	0.7	2.4	2.9	4.0	1.8	1.1	1.3	0.9	-0.5[f]
Bahamas	2.8	4.5	1.3	1.4	0.0	0.7	0.8	0.2	2.0	-0.3[f]
Barbados	4.7	7.3	4.4	6.5	9.6	2.4	1.1	2.3	-2.5	1.3[g]
Belize	4.1	4.4	-0.4	0.0	2.6	0.8	1.6	-0.2	-0.6	0.7
Dominica	6.0	2.0	3.2	0.3	1.9	1.3	-0.4	0.5	-0.5	-0.4[f]
Grenada	7.4	5.2	-2.3	4.2	3.5	1.8	-1.7	-0.2	1.1	1.9[f]
Guyana	14.1	6.4	3.6	4.5	3.3	3.4	0.9	1.2	-1.8	0.9
Jamaica	16.8	16.9	10.2	11.8	6.0	8.0	9.7	6.2	3.7	1.8
Saint Kitts and Nevis	2.9	6.5	1.2	4.3	2.0	0.5	0.6	-0.5	-2.4	-3.1[f]
Saint Lucia	6.8	3.4	-3.1	4.2	4.8	5.0	-0.7	3.7	-2.6	-4.1[f]
Saint Vincent and the Grenadines	8.3	8.7	-1.6	0.9	4.7	1.0	0.0	0.1	-2.1	0.9[f]
Suriname	8.3	9.4	1.3	10.3	15.3	4.4	0.6	3.9	25.2	77.1
Trinidad and Tobago	7.6	14.5	1.3	13.4	5.3	7.2	5.6	8.5	1.5	3.0

Source: Economic Commission for Latin America and the Caribbean (ECLAC), on the basis of official figures.
[a] Twelve-month variation to September 2016.
[b] Weighted average.
[c] Weighted average, does not include the Bolivarian Republic of Venezuela.
[d] Refers to national-currency markets.
[e] Up to 2008, national consumer price index.
[f] Twelve-month variation to June 2016.
[g] Twelve-month variation to May 2016.

Table A1.27
Latin America and the Caribbean: fiscal balances
(Percentages of GDP)

	Primary balance				Overall balance			
	2013	**2014**	**2015**	**2016**[a]	**2013**	**2014**	**2015**	**2016**[a]
Latin America and the Caribbean[b]	**-0.7**	**-0.4**	**-0.3**	**-0.3**	**-2.9**	**-2.7**	**-2.7**	**-2.8**
Latin America[c]	**-0.9**	**-1.0**	**-0.9**	**-0.8**	**-2.6**	**-2.8**	**-3.0**	**-3.0**
Argentina	-1.3	-2.3	-1.9	-2.7	-2.5	-4.2	-3.8	-5.0
Bolivia (Plurinational State of)[d]	2.0	-1.7	-3.6	...	1.4	-2.5	-4.5	...
Brazil	1.5	-0.3	-1.9	-2.8	-2.6	-5.1	-9.2	-7.9
Chile	-0.0	-1.0	-1.5	-2.3	-0.6	-1.6	-2.2	-3.0
Colombia	-0.1	-0.4	-0.8	-0.7	-2.3	-2.4	-3.0	-3.9
Costa Rica	-2.8	-3.1	-3.0	-2.6	-5.4	-5.7	-5.8	-5.5
Cuba	...	...	...	...	1.9	0.6	-0.4	...
Dominican Republic	-0.4	-0.1	0.3	0.2	-2.7	-2.6	-2.4	-2.7
Ecuador	-4.5	-4.9	-2.0	...	-5.7	-6.3	-3.8	...
El Salvador	0.6	0.8	1.3	2.4	-1.8	-1.6	-1.1	-0.2
Guatemala	-0.6	-0.4	0.1	-0.1	-2.1	-1.9	-1.4	-1.6
Haiti	-1.0	-0.5	0.3	0.8	-1.4	-0.9	0.1	0.6
Honduras	-5.8	-2.1	-0.6	-0.3	-7.9	-4.4	-3.0	-3.2
Mexico[e]	-0.5	-1.2	-1.3	-0.4	-2.3	-3.2	-3.5	-2.9
Nicaragua	1.0	0.6	0.3	0.2	0.1	-0.3	-0.6	-0.9
Panama	-1.9	-2.3	-2.1	-0.8	-3.8	-4.0	-3.9	-2.9
Paraguay	-1.4	-0.7	-1.2	-0.7	-1.7	-1.1	-1.8	-1.5
Peru[d]	1.8	0.8	-1.2	-1.8	0.7	-0.3	-2.2	-2.9
Uruguay	0.9	-0.1	-0.5	-0.5	-1.5	-2.3	-2.8	-3.0
Venezuela (Bolivarian Republic of)	...	...	...	...	...	...	...	...
The Caribbean[f]	**-0.7**	**0.6**	**0.7**	**0.7**	**-4.0**	**-2.7**	**-2.5**	**-2.5**
Antigua and Barbuda	-2.4	-0.1	4.6	2.5	-4.5	-2.7	2.1	0.0
Bahamas[g]	-3.1	-1.7	0.2	1.9	-5.6	-4.4	-3.0	-1.1
Barbados[h][i]	-4.1	0.7	0.1	-0.4	-11.2	-6.9	-7.5	-8.7
Belize[h]	0.9	-1.2	-4.7	1.0	-1.7	-3.8	-7.3	-1.7
Dominica	-7.4	0.4	0.0	-0.5	-9.4	-1.4	-1.8	-2.3
Grenada	-3.4	-1.2	2.2	3.7	-6.5	-4.7	-1.2	0.0
Guyana	-3.4	-4.5	-0.4	-3.7	-4.4	-5.5	-1.4	-4.6
Jamaica[h]	7.8	7.6	7.4	7.0	0.1	-0.5	-0.3	-1.0
Saint Kitts and Nevis	17.0	13.9	6.7	4.6	13.2	10.5	4.7	3.1
Saint Lucia	-3.0	0.2	1.4	1.6	-6.8	-3.7	-2.4	-2.4
Saint Vincent and the Grenadines	-3.7	-1.8	-0.7	-0.2	-6.2	-4.1	-2.9	-2.3
Suriname[j]	-3.2	-3.8	-7.7	-6.4	-6.0	-5.7	-10.0	-7.7
Trinidad and Tobago[k]	-1.4	-0.8	0.4	-2.5	-3.0	-2.5	-1.5	-4.2

Source: Economic Commission for Latin America and the Caribbean (ECLAC), on the basis of official figures.
[a] Preliminary figures established on the basis of information from official budgets and estimates.
[b] Simple averages for the 33 countries reported. Coverage corresponds to central government.
[c] Simple averages for 17 countries. Does not include Bolivarian Republic of Venezuela, Cuba or Plurinational State of Bolivia.
[d] General government.
[e] Federal public sector.
[f] Simple averages.
[g] Fiscal years, from 1 July to 30 June.
[h] Fiscal years, from 1 April to 31 March.
[i] Non-financial public sector.
[j] Includes statistical discrepancy.
[k] Fiscal years, from 1 October to 30 September.

Table A1.28
Latin America and the Caribbean: central government revenues composition
(Percentages of GDP)

	Total revenue				Tax revenue			
	2013	2014	2015	2016[a]	2013	2014	2015	2016[a]
Latin America and the Caribbean[b]	**22.8**	**22.8**	**22.8**	**22.9**	**17.8**	**18.0**	**18.3**	**18.1**
Latin America[c]	**17.9**	**17.8**	**17.8**	**17.6**	**14.8**	**14.8**	**15.1**	**14.9**
Argentina	19.9	20.6	20.7	19.5	17.5	17.3	17.6	16.6
Bolivia (Plurinational State of)[d]	36.7	37.7	36.1	...	21.7	22.3	23.2	...
Brazil	22.2	21.5	21.1	20.7	19.7	19.2	19.2	18.4
Chile	21.0	20.6	21.4	21.1	18.2	18.0	19.1	18.8
Colombia	16.9	16.6	16.1	14.8	14.2	14.3	14.5	14.0
Costa Rica	14.3	14.1	14.4	14.5	13.5	13.3	13.6	13.7
Cuba	43.1	31.3	34.2	...	22.3	19.4	...	...
Dominican Republic	14.4	14.8	14.5	14.1	13.7	13.8	13.5	13.0
Ecuador	21.4	19.9	20.3	...	14.4	14.1	15.6	...
El Salvador	16.3	15.8	16.0	16.4	15.4	15.1	15.2	15.6
Guatemala	11.6	11.5	10.8	11.0	11.0	10.8	10.2	10.3
Haiti	13.3	13.1	13.5	14.1	12.2	12.0	13.2	13.5
Honduras	17.0	18.7	19.5	19.4	15.1	16.7	17.7	17.7
Mexico[e]	23.6	23.1	23.4	24.3	9.7	10.5	13.0	13.5
Nicaragua	17.4	17.6	17.8	18.3	15.2	15.4	15.7	15.9
Panama	15.4	14.4	13.9	13.9	10.8	10.2	9.7	9.9
Paraguay	17.1	17.9	18.8	18.3	13.1	14.4	14.3	13.9
Peru[d]	22.4	22.3	20.3	19.4	19.0	19.2	17.5	16.9
Uruguay	20.7	20.0	19.6	19.7	18.2	17.7	17.6	17.7
Venezuela (Bolivarian Republic of)	...	...	...	...	...	...	...	...
The Caribbean[f]	**26.5**	**27.4**	**27.5**	**28.1**	**21.1**	**21.8**	**22.1**	**21.8**
Antigua and Barbuda	18.6	19.8	23.8	24.4	17.2	16.6	17.0	17.2
Bahamas[g]	17.0	19.7	21.3	23.6	14.6	17.4	19.2	20.5
Barbados[h][i]	27.3	28.8	29.2	30.9	25.2	26.7	27.5	29.1
Belize[h]	29.0	29.3	28.1	29.2	23.3	24.7	24.2	25.1
Dominica	27.9	31.8	31.0	33.4	22.1	22.1	23.6	24.3
Grenada	20.6	24.5	24.8	27.8	18.4	19.4	20.0	18.9
Guyana	23.6	23.6	25.8	26.5	20.6	21.4	21.9	21.0
Jamaica[h]	27.8	26.6	27.8	28.1	24.1	24.0	25.2	25.8
Saint Kitts and Nevis	46.2	43.4	39.8	...	19.8	20.7	21.5	...
Saint Lucia	24.8	25.7	26.2	...	22.9	22.9	23.6	...
Saint Vincent and the Grenadines	26.9	28.2	27.8	29.9	21.6	23.8	24.2	...
Suriname	23.3	21.7	19.3	18.9	18.5	16.5	15.4	14.6
Trinidad and Tobago[j]	31.0	33.4	32.0	26.0	26.2	27.1	23.6	16.9

Source: Economic Commission for Latin America and the Caribbean (ECLAC), on the basis of official figures.
[a] Preliminary figures established on the basis of information from official budgets and estimates.
[b] Simple averages for the 33 countries reported.
[c] Simple averages for 17 countries. Does not include Bolivarian Republic of Venezuela, Cuba or Plurinational State of Bolivia.
[d] General government.
[e] Federal public sector.
[f] Simple averages.
[g] Fiscal years, from 1 July to 30 June.
[h] Fiscal years, from 1 April to 31 March.
[i] Non-financial public sector.
[j] Fiscal years, from 1 October to 30 September.

Table A1.29
Latin America and the Caribbean: central government expenditure composition
(Percentages of GDP)

	Total expenditure				Interest payments on public debt				Capital expenditure			
	2013	2014	2015	2016[a]	2013	2014	2015	2016[a]	2013	2014	2015	2016[a]
Latin America and the Caribbean[b]	**25.6**	**25.4**	**25.5**	**25.6**	**2.3**	**2.4**	**2.5**	**2.5**	**5.2**	**5.0**	**4.5**	**4.5**
Latin America[c]	**20.5**	**20.6**	**20.7**	**20.5**	**1.7**	**1.8**	**2.0**	**2.1**	**4.3**	**4.0**	**3.8**	**3.5**
Argentina	22.4	24.8	24.5	24.5	1.2	1.9	1.8	2.4	2.8	4.2	2.7	2.1
Bolivia (Plurinational State of)[d]	35.4	40.2	40.6	...	0.6	0.8	0.9	...	13.5	16.6	13.8	...
Brazil	24.8	26.6	30.3	28.5	4.1	4.8	7.3	5.1	1.5	1.7	2.0	1.9
Chile	21.6	22.3	23.6	24.1	0.6	0.6	0.7	0.7	3.7	3.8	4.3	4.2
Colombia	19.2	19.0	19.2	18.7	2.2	2.1	2.2	3.1	3.1	3.0	3.0	1.9
Costa Rica	19.6	19.7	20.2	19.9	2.5	2.6	2.8	2.8	1.6	1.7	1.8	1.8
Cuba	41.1	30.7	34.6	...	...	...	...	...	7.4	3.1	4.0	...
Dominican Republic	17.1	17.3	16.9	16.8	2.3	2.5	2.7	2.9	3.3	2.7	2.8	2.3
Ecuador	27.2	26.2	24.1	...	1.2	1.4	1.8	...	12.2	11.5	9.6	...
El Salvador	18.1	17.4	17.1	16.7	2.4	2.4	2.4	2.6	3.0	2.8	2.6	2.4
Guatemala	13.8	13.4	12.3	12.6	1.6	1.4	1.6	1.5	3.0	2.9	2.2	2.4
Haiti	14.5	13.4	12.6	12.9	0.4	0.4	0.2	0.3	3.7	1.9	1.4	1.2
Honduras	24.9	23.1	22.6	22.6	2.1	2.3	2.5	3.0	5.2	5.2	4.7	5.7
Mexico[e]	26.0	26.3	26.9	27.2	1.9	1.9	2.2	2.5	5.4	5.2	5.1	5.9
Nicaragua	17.3	17.9	18.4	19.1	0.9	0.9	0.9	1.0	3.8	4.0	4.5	5.2
Panama	19.2	18.4	17.7	16.8	1.8	1.7	1.8	2.1	8.5	6.8	6.2	4.6
Paraguay	18.8	19.0	20.6	19.8	0.3	0.4	0.6	0.8	3.8	3.6	4.1	2.7
Peru[d]	21.7	22.6	22.5	22.3	1.1	1.1	1.0	1.1	6.2	6.0	5.5	5.3
Uruguay	22.2	22.3	22.4	22.7	2.4	2.3	2.3	2.5	1.4	1.4	1.2	1.2
Venezuela (Bolivarian Republic of)	...	...	...	...	...	...	...	...	...	...	...	...
The Caribbean[f]	**30.3**	**30.1**	**29.9**	**30.5**	**3.2**	**3.2**	**3.2**	**3.2**	**5.7**	**5.4**	**4.7**	**5.2**
Antigua and Barbuda	23.0	22.5	21.7	24.4	2.1	2.6	2.5	2.5	1.3	1.6	1.4	5.1
Bahamas[g]	22.7	24.2	24.3	24.7	2.5	2.7	3.1	3.0	3.0	3.3	2.0	2.6
Barbados[h i]	38.5	35.7	36.6	39.6	7.1	7.6	7.6	8.3	2.0	2.2	2.6	4.2
Belize[h]	30.7	33.1	35.4	30.9	2.7	2.5	2.6	2.7	6.8	8.6	9.8	5.1
Dominica	37.4	33.2	32.8	35.7	2.0	1.7	1.8	1.8	11.7	8.5	5.9	8.0
Grenada	27.1	29.2	26.0	27.8	3.1	3.5	3.4	3.7	6.8	9.2	8.4	10.5
Guyana	28.0	29.1	27.3	31.1	1.0	1.0	1.0	0.9	8.2	8.0	4.7	7.3
Jamaica[h]	27.6	27.1	28.1	29.1	7.7	8.1	7.7	8.0	2.6	1.5	2.0	2.5
Saint Kitts and Nevis	33.0	32.8	35.1	...	3.8	3.4	2.0	1.4	6.7	5.7	7.1	...
Saint Lucia	31.6	29.4	28.6	...	3.8	3.9	3.8	4.0	7.8	5.7	5.7	...
Saint Vincent and the Grenadines	33.0	32.3	30.7	32.2	2.5	2.3	2.2	2.2	7.8	6.4	5.0	4.4
Suriname	27.8	26.4	28.5	26.6	1.3	0.9	1.4	1.3	4.5	5.2	2.5	2.0
Trinidad and Tobago[j]	34.0	36.0	33.5	30.3	1.6	1.8	1.9	1.8	5.4	4.8	4.3	2.7

Source: Economic Commission for Latin America and the Caribbean (ECLAC), on the basis of official figures.
[a] Preliminary figures established on the basis of information from official budgets and estimates.
[b] Simple averages for the 33 countries reported.
[c] Simple averages for 17 countries. Does not include Bolivarian Republic of Venezuela, Cuba or Plurinational State of Bolivia.
[d] General government.
[e] Federal public-sector.
[f] Simple averages.
[g] Fiscal years, from 1 July to 30 June.
[h] Fiscal years, from 1 April to 31 March.
[i] Non-financial public sector.
[j] Fiscal years, from 1 October to 30 September.

Table A1.30
Latin America and the Caribbean: central government gross public debt
(Percentages of GDP)

	2007	2008	2009	2010	2011	2012	2013	2014	2015	2016[a]
Latin America and the Caribbean[b]	**42.9**	**41.6**	**45.3**	**45.5**	**45.6**	**47.4**	**48.9**	**49.6**	**50.7**	**50.8**
Latin America[b]	**30.3**	**28.8**	**30.9**	**29.8**	**29.0**	**30.5**	**32.3**	**33.6**	**36.5**	**37.9**
Argentina	44.4	39.2	39.6	36.1	33.3	35.1	43.3	44.4	53.6	54.0
Bolivia (Plurinational State of)	37.2	34.0	36.3	34.6	34.5	29.1	28.4	27.7	29.5	29.2
Brazil[c]	57.2	57.5	59.6	52.0	50.8	55.3	56.7	58.9	66.5	70.3
Chile	3.9	5.1	5.8	8.7	11.1	12.0	12.8	15.0	17.4	20.6
Colombia	36.6	36.2	38.1	38.7	36.5	34.6	37.2	40.0	43.9	44.6
Costa Rica	26.9	24.1	26.5	28.4	29.8	34.3	36.0	38.9	41.5	43.4
Dominican Republic	16.9	23.2	27.1	27.6	28.8	32.2	38.1	37.1	35.2	36.7
Ecuador	25.2	20.5	15.0	17.8	17.3	20.1	22.9	27.4	30.7	35.6
El Salvador	34.9	34.4	42.6	42.6	41.7	45.7	44.0	44.4	44.6	44.4
Guatemala	21.4	19.9	22.8	24.0	23.7	24.3	24.6	24.3	24.2	23.4
Haiti[d]	33.6	42.3	34.3	22.8	23.9	28.0	30.5	35.1	36.7	38.4
Honduras	17.4	20.1	23.9	30.4	32.5	35.4	43.8	45.6	45.2	45.9
Mexico[e]	20.6	24.0	27.2	27.2	27.5	28.2	29.8	31.7	34.4	36.7
Nicaragua	32.3	28.6	32.3	33.3	31.9	31.5	30.8	30.2	29.9	29.9
Panama	49.4	42.0	40.7	39.6	36.7	35.2	35.0	36.8	38.5	38.9
Paraguay	14.7	13.4	13.9	12.1	9.8	12.6	13.0	15.8	17.3	20.9
Peru	25.8	23.1	22.8	20.7	18.4	18.3	17.3	18.2	19.8	21.7
Uruguay	57.2	44.5	53.3	39.9	38.4	40.2	36.9	39.2	47.3	44.8
Venezuela (Bolivarian Republic of)	19.9	15.2	25.2	29.0	25.1	27.5	32.9	28.5	38.0	41.1
The Caribbean[b]	**61.2**	**60.4**	**66.4**	**68.6**	**69.7**	**72.2**	**73.1**	**72.9**	**71.5**	**69.6**
Antigua and Barbuda	85.8	73.8	80.8	74.3	77.1	71.9	77.7	82.7	70.0	66.9
Bahamas	36.9	37.4	50.2	54.3	55.4	59.6	65.6	72.9	75.1	74.0
Barbados	51.7	55.7	63.2	71.9	78.0	83.9	96.4	100.1	104.9	103.3
Belize	83.6	79.4	82.2	72.3	70.7	72.8	78.5	75.6	78.4	78.2
Dominica	67.0	59.4	53.1	56.7	54.6	64.6	64.2	64.3	66.1	66.2
Grenada	75.1	70.9	80.9	84.2	87.8	91.4	93.5	88.6	80.2	77.5
Guyana[f]	61.2	62.9	67.0	68.0	66.7	63.6	58.1	51.9	48.6	44.5
Jamaica[f]	110.9	112.3	126.3	131.7	131.4	133.9	135.5	131.8	127.3	124.2
Saint Kitts and Nevis	81.4	97.9	105.5	113.8	114.1	108.7	76.9	64.8	53.5	49.8
Saint Lucia	50.4	50.1	51.2	54.4	61.0	68.1	71.9	72.9	74.0	74.3
Saint Vincent and the Grenadines	48.0	45.8	51.0	55.6	58.5	61.2	63.6	68.3	66.8	65.2
Suriname	17.6	15.7	15.7	18.6	20.1	21.6	29.9	26.8	40.5	36.4
Trinidad and Tobago	26.5	23.8	36.3	36.1	30.9	36.9	37.9	47.2	43.7	44.2

Source: Economic Commission for Latin America and the Caribbean (ECLAC), on the basis of official figures.
[a] Preliminary figures.
[b] Simple averages.
[c] General government.
[d] Data to September 2013. Does not include public sector liabilities owed to commercial banks.
[e] Federal government.
[f] Public sector

Table A1.31
Latin America and the Caribbean: non-financial public sector gross public debt
(Percentages of GDP)

	2007	2008	2009	2010	2011	2012	2013	2014	2015	2016[a]
Latin America and the Caribbean[b]	**47.4**	**46.1**	**50.6**	**51.1**	**50.5**	**52.3**	**53.7**	**54.0**	**54.9**	**55.0**
Latin America[b]	**32.3**	**30.9**	**33.2**	**32.4**	**31.3**	**32.7**	**34.6**	**36.2**	**39.4**	**40.7**
Argentina	44.4	39.2	39.6	36.1	33.3	35.1	43.3	44.4	53.6	54.0
Bolivia (Plurinational State of)[c]	40.7	37.2	39.5	38.1	33.7	31.3	30.4	30.0	31.6	30.9
Brazil[d]	57.2	57.5	60.9	53.6	50.8	55.3	56.7	58.9	66.5	70.3
Chile	8.7	11.6	12.1	14.7	17.8	18.9	20.5	24.2	27.6	30.2
Colombia	43.8	42.6	45.1	46.2	43.1	40.7	43.1	46.0	50.1	50.3
Costa Rica	31.0	29.0	34.0	35.7	37.1	41.5	44.2	47.3	49.8	51.5
Dominican Republic[e]	16.9	23.2	27.1	27.6	28.8	32.2	38.1	37.1	35.2	36.7
Ecuador	27.1	22.1	16.3	19.6	18.3	21.1	24.0	29.5	32.7	38.4
El Salvador	37.0	36.9	45.2	45.1	44.1	47.9	46.3	46.7	47.3	47.2
Guatemala	21.6	20.1	23.3	24.4	23.9	24.5	24.7	24.5	24.3	23.5
Haiti[e f]	33.6	42.3	34.3	22.8	23.9	28.0	30.5	35.1	36.7	38.4
Honduras[e]	17.4	20.1	23.9	30.4	32.5	35.4	43.8	45.6	45.2	45.9
Mexico[g]	22.4	26.5	34.3	31.7	34.4	33.9	36.8	40.1	44.7	49.2
Nicaragua	32.9	29.4	34.2	34.8	32.6	32.2	31.5	30.7	30.4	30.3
Panama	50.0	42.6	45.4	43.0	37.3	35.7	35.5	37.1	38.8	39.2
Paraguay[h]	16.8	15.5	16.8	14.9	11.5	14.2	14.4	17.6	19.7	23.5
Peru	29.9	26.9	23.7	23.5	22.1	20.4	19.6	20.1	23.3	22.7
Uruguay	62.5	48.9	49.4	43.5	43.4	45.7	41.5	44.6	52.4	49.5
Venezuela (Bolivarian Republic of)[e]	19.9	15.2	25.2	29.0	25.1	27.5	32.9	28.5	38.0	41.1
The Caribbean[b]	**69.3**	**68.3**	**76.1**	**78.6**	**78.7**	**80.9**	**81.6**	**79.9**	**77.7**	**76.0**
Antigua and Barbuda	81.1	81.9	95.7	87.1	92.2	86.5	99.9	98.5	83.9	80.3
Bahamas[e]	36.9	37.4	50.2	54.3	55.4	59.6	65.6	72.9	75.1	74.0
Barbados	62.4	67.2	76.0	88.1	93.9	96.6	106.5	110.1	108.5	107.7
Belize	83.6	79.4	82.2	72.3	70.7	72.8	78.5	75.6	78.8	78.7
Dominica	81.2	72.6	66.4	73.1	67.5	77.6	76.7	75.7	78.3	78.5
Grenada	82.9	82.2	90.0	91.8	98.7	101.4	102.4	95.7	86.8	83.2
Guyana	61.2	62.9	67.0	68.0	66.7	63.6	58.1	51.9	48.6	44.5
Jamaica	110.9	112.3	126.3	131.7	131.4	133.9	135.5	131.8	127.3	124.2
Saint Kitts and Nevis	134.6	125.5	142.0	151.4	140.1	137.4	99.4	77.5	65.5	62.1
Saint Lucia	64.7	58.4	64.0	65.5	68.6	74.4	77.4	77.3	77.8	79.0
Saint Vincent and the Grenadines	55.5	58.0	64.7	66.7	69.9	72.8	75.8	79.9	78.5	77.9
Suriname[e]	17.6	15.7	15.7	18.6	20.1	21.6	29.9	26.8	40.5	36.4
Trinidad and Tobago	28.8	34.5	49.0	52.9	48.0	53.0	54.5	65.1	60.6	61.4

Source: Economic Commission for Latin America and the Caribbean (ECLAC), on the basis of official figures.
[a] Preliminary figures.
[b] Simple averages.
[c] Refers to the external debt of the non-financial public-sector and central-government domestic debt.
[d] General government.
[e] Data to September 2013. Does not include public sector liabilities owed to commercial banks.
[f] Central government.
[g] Federal public-sector.
[h] Domestic debt includes liabilities owed to the central bank only.

Publicaciones recientes de la CEPAL
ECLAC recent publications

www.cepal.org/publicaciones

Informes periódicos / *Annual reports*
También disponibles para años anteriores / *Issues for previous years also available*

- Estudio Económico de América Latina y el Caribe 2016, 242 p.
  Economic Survey of Latin America and the Caribbean 2016, 230 p.
- La Inversión Extranjera Directa en América Latina y el Caribe 2015, 150 p.
  Foreign Direct Investment in Latin America and the Caribbean 2015, 140 p.
- Anuario Estadístico de América Latina y el Caribe 2015 / *Statistical Yearbook for Latin America and the Caribbean 2015, 235 p.*
- Balance Preliminar de las Economías de América Latina y el Caribe 2015, 104 p.
  Preliminary Overview of the Economies of Latin America and the Caribbean 2015, 98 p.
- Panorama Social de América Latina 2015. Documento informativo, 68 p.
  Social Panorama of Latin America 2015. Briefing paper, 66 p.
- Panorama de la Inserción Internacional de América Latina y el Caribe 2015, 102 p.
  Latin America and the Caribbean in the World Economy 2015, 98 p.

Libros y documentos institucionales / *Institutional books and documents*

- 40 años de agenda regional de género, 2016, 130 p.
  40 years of the regional gender agenda, 128 p.
- La nueva revolución digital: de la Internet del consumo a la Internet de la producción, 2016, 100 p.
  The new digital revolution: From the consumer Internet to the industrial Internet, 2016, 100 p.
- Panorama fiscal de América Latina y el Caribe 2016: las finanzas públicas ante el desafío de conciliar austeridad con crecimiento e igualdad, 2016, 90 p.
- Reflexiones sobre el desarrollo en América Latina y el Caribe: conferencias magistrales 2015, 2016, 74 p.
- Panorama Económico y Social de la Comunidad de Estados Latinoamericanos y Caribeños, 2015, 58 p.
  Economic and Social Panorama of the Community of Latin American and Caribbean States 2015, 56 p.
- Desarrollo social inclusivo: una nueva generación de políticas para superar la pobreza y reducir la desigualdad en América Latina y el Caribe, 2015, 180 p.
  Inclusive social development: The next generation of policies for overcoming poverty and reducing inequality in Latin America and the Caribbean, 2015, 172 p.
- Guía operacional para la implementación y el seguimiento del Consenso de Montevideo sobre Población y Desarrollo, 2015, 146 p.
  Operational guide for implementation and follow-up of the Montevideo Consensus on Population and Development, 2015, 139 p.
- América Latina y el Caribe: una mirada al futuro desde los Objetivos de Desarrollo del Milenio. Informe regional de monitoreo de los Objetivos de Desarrollo del Milenio (ODM) en América Latina y el Caribe, 2015, 88 p.
  Latin America and the Caribbean: Looking ahead after the Millennium Development Goals. Regional monitoring report on the Millennium Development Goals in Latin America and the Caribbean, 2015, 88 p.
- La nueva revolución digital: de la Internet del consumo a la Internet de la producción, 2015, 98 p.
  The new digital revolution: From the consumer Internet to the industrial Internet, 2015, 98 p.
- Globalización, integración y comercio inclusivo en América Latina. Textos seleccionados de la CEPAL (2010-2014), 2015, 326 p.
- El desafío de la sostenibilidad ambiental en América Latina y el Caribe. Textos seleccionados de la CEPAL (2012-2014), 2015, 148 p.
- Pactos para la igualdad: hacia un futuro sostenible, 2014, 340 p.
  Covenants for Equality: Towards a sustainable future, 2014, 330 p.

- Cambio estructural para la igualdad: una visión integrada del desarrollo, 2012, 330 p.
  Structural Change for Equality: An integrated approach to development, 2012, 308 p.

- La hora de la igualdad: brechas por cerrar, caminos por abrir, 2010, 290 p.
  Time for Equality: Closing gaps, opening trails, 2010, 270 p.
  A Hora da Igualdade: Brechas por fechar, caminhos por abrir, 2010, 268 p.

Libros de la CEPAL / *ECLAC books*

139 Hacia una nueva gobernanza de los recursos naturales en América Latina y el Caribe, Hugo Altomonte, Ricardo J. Sánchez, 2016, 256 p.

138 Estructura productiva y política macroeconómica: enfoques heterodoxos desde América Latina, Alicia Bárcena Ibarra, Antonio Prado, Martín Abeles (eds.), 2015, 282 p.

137 Juventud: realidades y retos para un desarrollo con igualdad, Daniela Trucco, Heidi Ullmann (eds.), 2015, 282 p.

136 Instrumentos de protección social: caminos latinoamericanos hacia la universalización, Simone Cecchini, Fernando Filgueira, Rodrigo Martínez, Cecilia Rossel (eds.), 2015, 510 p.

135 *Rising concentration in Asia-Latin American value chains: Can small firms turn the tide?, Osvaldo Rosales, Keiji Inoue, Nanno Mulder (eds.), 2015, 282 p.*

134 Desigualdad, concentración del ingreso y tributación sobre las altas rentas en América Latina, Juan Pablo Jiménez (ed.), 2015, 172 p.

Copublicaciones / *Co-publications*

- El imperativo de la igualdad, Alicia Bárcena, Antonio Prado, CEPAL/Siglo Veintiuno, Argentina, 2016, 244 p.

- Gobernanza global y desarrollo: nuevos desafíos y prioridades de la cooperación internacional, José Antonio Ocampo (ed.), CEPAL/Siglo Veintiuno, Argentina, 2015, 286 p.

- *Decentralization and Reform in Latin America: Improving Intergovernmental Relations, Giorgio Brosio and Juan Pablo Jiménez (eds.), ECLAC/Edward Elgar Publishing, United Kingdom, 2012, 450 p.*

- Sentido de pertenencia en sociedades fragmentadas: América Latina desde una perspectiva global, Martín Hopenhayn y Ana Sojo (comps.), CEPAL/Siglo Veintiuno, Argentina, 2011, 350 p.

Coediciones / *Co-editions*

- Perspectivas económicas de América Latina 2016: hacia una nueva asociación con China, 2015, 240 p.
  Latin American Economic Outlook 2016: Towards a new Partnership with China, 2015, 220 p.

- Perspectivas de la agricultura y del desarrollo rural en las Américas: una mirada hacia América Latina y el Caribe 2015-2016, CEPAL/FAO/IICA, 2015, 212 p.

Documentos de proyecto / *Project documents*

- Complejos productivos y territorio en la Argentina: aportes para el estudio de la geografía económica del país, 2015, 216 p.

- Las juventudes centroamericanas en contextos de inseguridad y violencia: realidades y retos para su inclusión social, Teresita Escotto Quesada, 2015, 168 p.

- La economía del cambio climático en el Perú, 2014, 152 p.

Cuadernos estadísticos de la CEPAL

44 Las cuentas de los hogares y el bienestar en América Latina. Más allá del PIB, 2016.

43 Estadísticas económicas de América Latina y el Caribe: Aspectos metodológicos y resultados del cambio de año base de 2005 a 2010

Series de la CEPAL / *ECLAC Series*

Asuntos de Género / Comercio Internacional / Desarrollo Productivo / Desarrollo Territorial / Estudios Estadísticos / Estudios y Perspectivas (Bogotá, Brasilia, Buenos Aires, México, Montevideo) / *Studies and Perspectives* (The Caribbean, Washington) / Financiamiento del Desarrollo / Gestión Pública / Informes y Estudios Especiales / Macroeconomía del Desarrollo / Medio Ambiente y Desarrollo / Población y Desarrollo / Política Fiscal / Políticas Sociales / Recursos Naturales e Infraestructura / Seminarios y Conferencias.

Manuales de la CEPAL

3 Manual de formación regional para la implementación de la resolución 1325 (2000) del Consejo de Seguridad de las Naciones Unidas relativa a las mujeres, la paz y la seguridad, María Cristina Benavente R., Marcela Donadio, Pamela Villalobos, 2016, 126 p.

2 Guía general para la gestión de residuos sólidos domiciliarios, Estefani Rondón Toro, Marcel Szantó Narea, Juan Francisco Pacheco, Eduardo Contreras, Alejandro Gálvez, 2016, 212 p.

1 La planificación participativa para lograr un cambio estructural con igualdad: las estrategias de participación ciudadana en los procesos de planificación multiescalar, Carlos Sandoval, Andrea Sanhueza, Alicia Williner, 2015, 74 p.

Revista CEPAL / *CEPAL Review*

La Revista se inició en 1976, con el propósito de contribuir al examen de los problemas del desarrollo socioeconómico de la región. La *Revista CEPAL* se publica en español e inglés tres veces por año.

CEPAL Review first appeared in 1976, its aim being to make a contribution to the study of the economic and social development problems of the region. CEPAL Review is published in Spanish and English versions three times a year.

Observatorio demográfico / *Demographic Observatory*

Edición bilingüe (español e inglés) que proporciona información estadística actualizada, referente a estimaciones y proyecciones de población de los países de América Latina y el Caribe. Desde 2013 el Observatorio aparece una vez al año.

Bilingual publication (Spanish and English) proving up-to-date estimates and projections of the populations of the Latin American and Caribbean countries. Since 2013, the Observatory appears once a year.

Notas de población

Revista especializada que publica artículos e informes acerca de las investigaciones más recientes sobre la dinámica demográfica en la región. También incluye información sobre actividades científicas y profesionales en el campo de población. La revista se publica desde 1973 y aparece dos veces al año, en junio y diciembre.

Specialized journal which publishes articles and reports on recent studies of demographic dynamics in the region. Also includes information on scientific and professional activities in the field of population. Published since 1973, the journal appears twice a year in June and December.

Las publicaciones de la CEPAL están disponibles en:
ECLAC publications are available at:

www.cepal.org/publicaciones

También se pueden adquirir a través de:
They can also be ordered through:

www.un.org/publications

United Nations Publications
PO Box 960
Herndon, VA 20172
USA

Tel. (1-888)254-4286
Fax (1-800)338-4550
Contacto / *Contact*: publications@un.org
Pedidos / *Orders*: order@un.org